ELECTRONIC SIGNATURES

Authentication Technology
from a Legal Perspective

For other titles in the Series see p. 150

INFORMATION TECHNOLOGY & LAW SERIES ⑤

ELECTRONIC SIGNATURES

Authentication Technology from a Legal Perspective

M.H.M. Schellekens

*Center for Law, Public Administration and Informatization
Tilburg University*

T•M•C•ASSER PRESS
The Hague

The *Information Technology & Law Series* is published
for IT*e*R by T·M·C·ASSER PRESS
P.O. Box 16163, 2500 BD The Hague, The Netherlands
<www.asserpress.nl>

T·M·C·ASSER PRESS English language books are distributed exclusively by:

Cambridge University Press, The Edinburgh Building, Shaftesbury Road,
Cambridge CB2 2RU, UK,
or
for customers in the USA, Canada and Mexico:
Cambridge University Press, 40 West 20th Street, New York, NY 10011-4211, USA

<www.cambridge.org>

The *Information Technology & Law Series* is an initiative of IT*e*R, the National Programme for Information Technology and Law, which is a research programme set up by the Dutch government and the Netherlands Organisation for Scientific Research (NWO) in The Hague. Since 1995 IT*e*R has published all of its research results in its own book series. In 2002 IT*e*R launched the present internationally orientated and English language *Information Technology & Law Series*. This series deals with the implications of information technology for legal systems and institutions. It is not restricted to publishing IT*e*R's research results. Hence, authors are invited and encouraged to submit their manuscripts for inclusion. Manuscripts and related correspondence can be sent to the Series' Editorial Office, which will also gladly provide more information concerning editorial standards and procedures.

Editorial Office
NWO / IT*e*R
P.O. Box 93461
2509 AL The Hague, The Netherlands
Tel. +31(0)70-3440950; Fax +31(0)70-3832841
E-mail: <iter@nwo.nl>
Web site: <www.nwo.nl/iter>

Single copies or Standing Order
The books in the *Information Technology & Law Series* can either be purchased as single copies at the regular retail price or through a standing order at a discount. For ordering information see the information on top of this page or visit the publisher's web site at <www.asserpress.nl/cata/itlaw5/fra.htm>.

ISBN 90-6704-174-2
ISSN 1570-2782

Cover and lay-out: Oasis Productions, Nieuwerkerk a/d IJssel, The Netherlands
Printing and binding: Koninklijke Wöhrmann BV, Zutphen, The Netherlands

TABLE OF CONTENTS

ABBREVIATIONS

ABA	American Bankers Association
ACL	Access Control List
ADR	Alternative Dispute Resolution
AES	Advanced Encryption Standard
ANSI	American Natonal Standard Institute
ATM	Automatic teller machine
BBL	Bolero Bill of Lading
CA	Certification Authority
CMI	Comité Maritime Internationale
CPS	Certification Practise Statement
CRC	Cyclic Redundancy Check
CRL	Certificate Revocation List
CSP	Certification Service Provider
DCC	Dutch Civil Code
DCCP	Dutch Code of Civil Procedure
DES	Data Encryption Standard
DHCP	Dynamic Host Configuration Protocol
DNS	Domain Name Server
DOI	Digital object identifier
DSA	Digital Signature Algorithm
DSS	Digital Signature Standard
DTD	Document Type Declaration
EDI	Electronic Data Interchange
ETSI	European Telecommunications Standard Institute
FIPS	Federal Information Processing Standard
HR	Hoge Raad

ICT   Information and Communication Technology
ID   Identification number
IETF   The Internet Engineering Task Force
IMAP   Internet Message Access Protocol
IP   Internet Protocol
ISDN   Integrated Services Digital Network

JILT   Journal of Information Law & Technology

KPN   The main (incumbant) Dutch telecom operator
Ktg.   Dutch Summary Court (Kantongerecht)

LAN   Local Area Network

MAC   Message Autentication Code ch. 2
MAC address   Media Access Layer address
MIME   Multipurpose Internet Mail Extensions
MOSS   MIME Object Security Services

NJ   Dutch case law reference
NJB   Nederlands Juristenblad
NRD   Non-Refutable Document

ODR   On-line Dispute Resolution

PEM   Privacy Enhanced Mail
PIN   Personal Identification Number
PGP   Pretty Good Privacy
PKI   Public Key Infrastructure

RA   Registering Authority
RIPE   Réseau IP Européen
RSA   Encryption method (by Rivest, Shamir and Adleman)
RvdW   Rechtspraak van de week

SCOS   Smartcard operating system
SET   Secure Electronic Transactions

SDSI	Simple Distributed Security Infrastructure
SIDN	Stichting Internet Domein Namen
SKIP	Simple Key Management for Internet Protocols
SPKI	Simple Public Key Infrastructure
SSL	Secure Socket Layer
S2ML	Security Service Markup Language
TCP	Transmission Control Protocol
TLS	Transport Layer Security
TSA	Time Stamping Authority
TTP	Trusted third party
UNCITRAL	UN Commission on International Trade Law
URI	Uniform Resource Identifier
URL	Uniform Resource Locator
URN	Uniform Resource Name
USB	Universal Serial Bus
WORM	Write Once Read Many
WPNR	Weekblad voor Privaatrecht, Notariaat en Registratie
WTLS	Wireless Transport Layer Security
WWW	World Wide Web
XML	eXtensible Markup Language

Chapter 1
INTRODUCTION

Chapter 1
INTRODUCTION

1.1 INTRODUCTION

In the ITeR Series of books in 2000 there appeared a book entitled Digital Signature Blindness.[1] It deals primarily with the legislative techniques for bringing electronic signatures within the ambit of the law. From this research it appeared that knowledge concerning authentication technology among legal professionals is still somewhat marginal, despite the coverage that the subject has had in recent years. That provided the idea for this book that sets out to describe the main features of authentication technologies.

However, a description of the authentication technologies alone will barely be interesting for the legally educated reader, without an indication of what such technology can be used for. That provided the stepping-stone to the second part of this research: viz., to discover what the usability of authentication technology entails for its users.

Usability is now a very wide concept, encompassing various legal and non-legal aspects such as user friendliness, consumer acceptation, the spread of use, technical compatibility, etc. In this book usability is approached from a legal perspective. Within this legal perspective, authentication technology is defined as being usable if the users of the technology are able to correctly foresee the legal consequences that the use of the technology entails. The users are both the signatories and the persons relying on a signature. Possible trusted third parties are not considered to be users of the technology.

---

[1] Aalberts and van der Hof 2000. The research for this book took place at the Center for Law, Public Administration and Informatization of the Faculty of Law of Tilburg University.

1.2   DEFINING THE PROBLEM

The central problem that is to be addressed in this book is the following:

What kinds of authentication technologies exist? What is their usability from a legal perspective, more specifically what is the legal certainty with which signatures can be used?

All the legal questions are dealt with according to Dutch law, unless indicated otherwise. As has been said above, usability is here taken to mean that an user can foresee what the legal consequences are of the use of authentication technology. The legal consequences of the use of authentication technology can be differentiated between the intended consequences of the use of authentication technology and the more secondary effects that the use of electronic signatures can have. The first category deals with the question of how good an electronic signature is in performing its primary functionality. In this book, the following legal areas of functionality are distinguished:

- Can an electronic signature be qualified as a signature under the law?
- What is the evidentiary value of an electronic signature, or at least a document signed with the aid of an electronic signature?

In the second category, one finds consequences that were not (or not primarily) intended by the user or users, but may be seen as a side-effect of the use of authentication technology, such as the consequences of an abuse of authentication technology. In the second category, the following areas are discerned:

- How are the risks divided between the parties involved (especially the users), if somebody makes an unauthorised use of somebody else's electronic signature?
- What is the division of the burden of proof in such a case?
- What are the most pressing implications for the informational privacy of the holders of electronic signatures?

With these issues the subject of legal usability is not completely covered. Enforcement is perhaps the most obvious issue that is not dealt with. Therefore I will indicate for what reason enforcement has been omitted as a separate issue.

This has the following background. A signature may alleviate evidentiary burdens that may arise when enforcing a contract, but enforcing a contract involves much more than evidence of the existence and contents of a contract. E-commerce has opened the possibility to engage in cross-border business with a low value per transaction. Even if one has the authenticated identity of one's contracting party, it may still be too complicated or expensive to commence legal proceedings against a party. A signature does not in itself result in compliance with contracts and legal rules. A digital signature may, however, be an important part of a more encompassing enforcement concept. The security dimension of signatures only makes sense if one is really willing to embark upon enforcement (instead of accepting the loss). Enforcement in the Internet environment is not something that can be done on an *ad hoc* basis. The territorial division of the law hampers enforcement in the borderless Internet environment: each country has its own system for determining and administering law. Furthermore, traditional courts are not as yet tailored to the enforcement needs that originate from the Internet. Alternative Dispute Resolution (hereinafter: ADR) and On-line Dispute Resolution (Hereinafter: ODR) may bring some solutions. ADR and ODR that are tailored to the needs of the on-line environment are however only in their formative stages. When the resolution of disputes that originate on the Internet has become more accessible, be it through ADR and ODR or by means of the traditional courts, the value of digital signatures as a link in the enforcement chain may become more apparent. So the question of enforcement covers a much wider area and this cannot be sensibly dealt with in a book solely on electronic signatures.

The research for this book is based on literature study and qualitative interviews with experts. A list of experts can be found in the appendix.

1.3 OUTLINE

The second chapter will provide an overview of the authentication technologies that are available at this moment in time. The overview is not confined to authentication technologies that are designated as such. Also technologies for identification within the Internet will be dealt with. These technologies are included because they may fulfil certain functions of 'real' authentication technologies. To a certain extent they may thus be used as a substitute for those technologies. The lack of functionality that they may demonstrate is compensated by their omnipresence. Furthermore, they are available at no extra cost to most people.

The third chapter will deal with the usability of electronic signatures from the perspective that their usability depends on how good they are in fulfilling the functions for which they are used. As indicated above, two issues will be dealt with: the qualifiability of an electronic signature as a signature under the law and the evidentiary value of electronic signatures. In order to deal with the first issue the functions which a signature has under the law have been analysed. Based on this analysis, the suitability of the technologies described in the second chapter as 'signatures' has been explored. Extra attention is paid to the function of 'originality' because it cannot very well be emulated by the typical authentication technologies and thus requires a broader approach.

The fourth chapter is dedicated to more secondary concerns of usability that do not directly concern the ordinary use of electronic signatures. The first issue dealt with is liability in the case of an unauthorised use of electronic signatures: who bears the risk for unauthorised uses of an electronic signature when the damage cannot be recovered from the unauthorised user? A second issue concerns the division of the burden of proof with respect to compromises of signatures or the documents they are attached to.

The fifth chapter deals with some issues of informational privacy in relation to electronic signatures. The fact that a signature identifies the signatory brings signatures within the realm of informational privacy. Although it seems to be an inherent feature of signatures that they involve identification, one has to bear in mind that the electronic form of the electronic signature makes it easier to process signature information. The position of the signatory may thus weaken in relation to the position of those parties which rely thereon. Furthermore, a wide availability of electronic signatures may encourage such signatures to be used in situations that are presently dealt with without signatures.

The sixth chapter is the conclusion in which no new facts are presented. The lines traced in the previous chapters are here brought together and this chapter can be seen as a résumé of the entire book.

Chapter 2
AUTHENTICATION TECHNOLOGY:
AN ELEMENTARY EXPLANATION

Chapter 2
AUTHENTICATION TECHNOLOGY:
AN ELEMENTARY EXPLANATION

2.1   INTRODUCTION

In this chapter, the elementary functioning of authentication technologies is explained. The first section focuses on mechanisms for identifying hardware, data and users within the Internet that are indispensable for its functioning. In their conception their legal significance was of little or no importance. The following section focuses on dedicated means of authentication other than digital signatures. The third section deals with digital signatures, PKIs and their applications. Finally, some remaining subjects are touched upon. Timestamps and cards are in themselves not authentication technologies, but form useful additional functionalities, warranting their coverage in this chapter.

2.2   AUTHENTICATION WITHIN THE INTERNET

Computer networks such as the Internet already contain many ways of identifying persons, equipment or data. These mechanisms are often designed with functionality in mind. Resistance against manipulation by malevolent parties is only a secondary concern, or even not a concern at all. Nonetheless, in practice many of these technologies are relied upon for authentication purposes. For instance, contracts are being concluded by e-mail, purchases are being made on web sites with familiar sounding domain names. People who receive an e-mail message seldom think of the possibility that the person that is indicated as the sender might not – as a consequence of some manipulation – be the actual sender of the message. Because of the way in which these mechanisms are often used, they are dealt with here,

M.H.M. Schellekens, Electronic Signatures
© 2004, ITeR, The Hague, and the author

although they were not designed with signature-like authentication in mind. The following technologies with identification potential are dealt with: the MAC address, the IP address, the domain name, the e-mail address, and the URI.

In a LAN, a computer is designated by its MAC address (Media Access Layer).[2] The system administrator knows which computer has which MAC address. This MAC is only significant within the LAN, however, and only plays a role at the technical level. Therefore, the MAC address will hereinafter not be dealt with.

Within the Internet, computers are being identified by their IP address. Packets sent over the Internet have a so-called IP header. The header fulfils a function that is comparable to that of an envelope in traditional mail: in the header the IP addresses of both the sender and the receiver of the packet are mentioned. In Europe RIPE (Réseau IP Européen) allocates IP addresses to companies, organisations and Internet Service Providers, who can then assign them to computers. RIPE runs a database containing IP addresses and the entities to which the IP addresses have been granted.[3] This database is accessible to the public. To some extent, IP addresses might thus serve as tools for identifying persons, companies and organisations. There are, however, a few drawbacks that limit the usability of IP addresses as a tool for discovering somebody's identity. The entities to which IP addresses are being allocated may sub-allocate them to other persons, companies or organisations, thus complicating the search for the 'owner' of an IP address. Secondly, an IP address cannot only be statically bound to a computer, it might also be done dynamically. If this is done statically the computer is known under the IP address on a less or more permanent basis.[4] Using, for instance, the Dynamic Host Configuration Protocol (hereinafter: DHCP), it is possible to bind an IP address to a computer for the duration of a session. After the termination of the session the IP address might be allocated to another computer.

---

[2] Vanheste 1997, pp. 23-24.

[3] The database is accessible through the Internet <http://www.ripe.net/perl/whois>, accessed in 2001.

[4] It is possible to grant an IP address that is statically bound to a certain computer to another computer, but it will take some time before routers in the Internet have been adjusted to the new situation.

An Internet Access provider can, for example, grant an IP address to a subscriber for the duration of a surfing session. Once the subscriber logs off, the IP address is freed and can be made available to some other subscriber. Tracing who has actually used an IP address (and thus, arguably, a certain computer), is then only possible if one has at one's disposal the loggings of the DHCP server and the times at which the session took place. And, thirdly, one is generally interested in knowing who used a computer at a certain point in time. This person might be quite different from the person in whose name an IP address is registered or the person who is discovered to be using (DHCP) loggings.

Fourthly, the authentication of the sender on the basis of the indication of the sender's IP address in the header is vulnerable to a so-called spoofing attack. This means that an attacker substitutes his own IP address in the header of a packet for that of somebody else. Usually he expects to gain access to a system that grants access based on IP authentication.

As IP addresses are difficult to memorise, it has been made possible to allocate names, so-called domain names, to computers that already have IP addresses. The Stichting Internet Domein Namen (hereinafter: SIDN) allocates, for example, domain names in the '.nl' country code Top level Domain. Just like its sister and parent organisations, SIDN runs a database containing domain names and the names of the persons, companies and organisations to which domain names have been granted. The SIDN database is accessible to the public at the URL: <http://www.sidn.nl/bestaat.lp>. A Domain name might thus also serve as a tool for identification.[5]

An e-mail address can serve as a means to identify a person. An e-mail address is after all often allocated to a particular person. There are, however, a number of circumstances that limit e-mail addresses' capacity to identify. In the first place, an e-mail address can be a so-called functional mail name; a functional mail name refers to somebody in a specific function, e.g., webmaster@...nl. It does not refer to a particular person. Sec-

---

[5] Apart from the fact that domain names are registered in somebody's (a natural or legal person's) name, another method of identification is possible. Through a Domain Name Server (hereinafter: DNS), it is possible to find the IP address that is associated with a domain name. Through a database such as RIPE's it is possible to find in whose name the IP address is registered.

ondly, the part of an e-mail address preceding the '@' can sometimes be freely chosen. It is therefore possible to choose an e-mail address that conveys a suggestion of identity that is not in accordance with reality. Thirdly, by using an anonymous remailer, the sender of an e-mail address can easily hide his true e-mail address from the recipient of the message. Apart from these cases that represent legitimate uses, there can also be malevolent uses of e-mail addresses. The sender of a message or a third party may change the sender's e-mail address into another e-mail address; this is called spoofing.

Apart from these circumstances, it cannot be denied, however, that e-mail addresses often identify persons in the course of their daily use. Even more so, this identifying capability to a large extent determines the attractiveness and the usability of e-mail. E-mail is, after all, the most used means of person-to-person communication within the Internet.

A Uniform Resource Identifier (hereinafter: URI) is the generic name for all types of names and addresses that refer to objects on the World Wide Web.[6] A Uniform Resource Locator (hereinafter: URL) or a Uniform Resource Name (hereinafter: URN) is an example of a URI. An URL points to an object by specifying the network location, where the object on the WWW can be found. An URN refers to the objects themselves irrespective of the Web address where they reside. An URI generally only identifies data objects, and not persons using a computer.

Apart from the identity of communicating parties, the integrity of the message is relevant for authentication purposes as well. To check the integrity of messages sent through the Internet a checksum, such as a Cyclic Redundancy Check (hereinafter: CRC) can be added to a message. The sender of the message calculates the checksum and sends it along with the message. After reception the recipient will calculate the checksum anew. If, during the transmission of the message, one or more bits of the message have become corrupted, the checksum calculated after the reception of the message will not equal the checksum that was sent along with the message. This inequality signals to the recipient that the integrity of the message has been affected. He can then take appropriate action, such as requesting the renewed sending of the message. This tech-

---

[6] This definition is taken from webopedia.com.

nology is only meant to detect infractions of message integrity that have technical causes. If it is used to detect man-made infractions it exhibits a shortcoming. Somebody who wilfully manipulates the contents of a message while in transit can easily calculate a new checksum that is in accordance with the message in its manipulated form. If the manipulator replaces the old checksum with the new one, a verification of the integrity of the message by the recipient will reveal nothing about the manipulation. Hereinafter, it will be explained that this problem can be overcome by using keyed checksums.

The technologies dealt with in this section show marked deficiencies for use as signatures. Identifying information often primarily identifies equipment (IP address, Domain name) or data (URI). It may be possible to find out in whose name the equipment or data are registered. But that might not shed light on the identity of the user of the equipment or data. Furthermore, the use of such technology does not imply the 'authentication' of the messages sent. The technologies offer little or no protection against manipulation by third persons (think, for instance, of e-mail spoofing or recalculation of CRCs). They do have advantages, however, such as their wide availability, enabling almost everybody to make use of them. Furthermore, in daily life the correctness of their functioning is often relied upon.

2.3   DEDICATED MEANS OF AUTHENTICATION

More readily associated with the idea of authentication, are techniques that offer some sort of assurance against manipulation. Although manipulations may take place in various ways, one of the most prominent problems to be addressed is how to ensure that the person 'sitting at the keyboard' is who he claims to be and is authorised to do what he claims to be entitled to. This 'authentication' of the person can generally be based on something that the person knows, on something that he is or on something that he possesses. The word 'authentication' is used here in its meaning of verification of identity or authority.

Possession or something one has

The scanned handwritten signature: A handwritten signature is scanned into a computer memory. Signing only involves 'pasting' the graphical image of the signature in the document that is to be signed. It goes without saying that this is an unsafe technology. Anybody with access to a signed document can copy the signature and sign documents with the signatory's signature at will. In general, one can say that digital data as opposed to physical objects can easily be reproduced; the reproduction entails the risk that possession is no longer exclusive. The possession of data is therefore less suitable as a means for verifying the identity or authority of the 'person sitting at the keyboard'.

As examples of physical objects used for authentication purposes, dongles and cards can be mentioned. A dongle is a hardware device that is attached to a computer and controls the access to a resource, mostly a software application. In a PC a dongle is often connected to the parallel port. The use of the resource guarded by the dongle is therefore restricted to possessors of the dongle and persons having access to a computer that is equipped with the dongle. Since persons usually do not carry a dongle with them, much of the access control comes to depend on the access to the room where the computer is located.

The most important examples of authentication by possession are electromagnetic cards and smart cards. They are often handed out to particular persons, who are to keep the cards to themselves. Often functionalities on the card or in the network support and strengthen the authentication. In the fourth section of this chapter, cards will be dealt with more extensively.

Biometrics or something one is

Biometrics is the technology for measuring and analysing characteristics of a human body. These characteristics may be physiological or behavioural characteristics. Examples of physiological characteristics are: the fingerprint, iris and retinal patterns, hand geometry and facial characteristics. Technologies based on behavioural characteristics are the dynamic signature, keystroke analysis and voice recognition. As an example, I will here describe dynamic signatures. There are several manufacturers of pens with which personal characteristics can be measured and recorded during signing: e.g., LCI – the product is called Smartpen – and CyberSIGN.[7] The pen which is used is a pen with which a normal handwritten signature can be made on a special pad or sometimes on paper (e.g., in the case of the Smartpen). The way in which the signatory signs is measured. This is done by measuring, for example, the speed with which the signature is made, the angle at which the pen is held in the hand and the pressure that is exercised while signing; the changes in these values during the act of signing are of course also measured. This yields the so-called life scan, i.e., the recording of certain characteristics of the signatory in a template. The template is encrypted and transmitted to the signatory's computer through a wire or wireless. The signatory's computer may itself verify the 'signature' or it may, through a secure connection, contact a secured database that performs the verification. The verification takes place by matching the life scan against reference templates. In the database, such a reference template is related to identifying or authorising information concerning the person whose characteristics are laid down in the template. The technology often also generates a digital file containing the graphical image of the signature. This image can then be pasted into a document. One must however bear in mind that the 'strength' of the technology is not in this image: the mentioned characteristics of the act of signing are relevant and not so much the end result: the graphical image of the signature.

The technology can be used for various applications in which the identity or authorisations of a user need to be established. An example is the use of the technology as a 'guard' for access to a private key of a digital signature; the meaning of the concept 'private key' will be explained hereinafter. Another example is the use of dynamic signatures by employees for checking whether a 'signing' employee is authorised to perform the transaction he is about to enter into. The technology can also be used for the conclusion of high value contracts at a distance. The technology can give assurance in real time that the 'other' party actually signed. The applications mentioned concern (access) decisions that have to be taken in real time.

It is also possible that a 'signature' is generated that can be appended to a document. Figure 1 provides an example of such a signature. In this

---

[7] See for instance the LCI Smartpen.

Figure 1

An example of a CyberSIGN 'signature'. The status field indicates that the signature is not valid. This may be the case because the user failed to indicate the purpose for signing or because the verification of the live scan has not yet taken place. Once the purpose is indicated, the signature can be verified and – if all is well – appended to the Word-document that has been signed.

case, it is a signature made with the help of CyberSIGN for Word NRD (Non-Refutable Document). On the left, the signature image can be seen. On the right, the verification status of the signature, the user ID of the signatory, the 'identity' of the CyberSIGN secure server, a timestamp and the purpose for which the signature was made are (or can be) indicated. Once the signature is appended to the document a checksum is calculated over the document and the signature together. If the document is altered after the signature has been appended the checksum will reveal the alteration. In such a case, the CyberSIGN software will remove the appended signature from the document.

As physiological and behavioural characteristics may change over time or become damaged (e.g., a cut to a finger) biometric verification is not based upon exact matches, but rather on probable matches. Even if a life scan slightly differs from the reference data, verification may still result in a probable match. Often the margins of tolerable divergence can be attuned. If too narrow margins are chosen, the use of the biometric system will result in false rejections, often resulting in user irritation. If they are too wide, verification may result in false acceptances, which in turn compromises security. Biometric technology is, as yet, not so far advanced that both false rejection and false acceptance can be totally excluded.

Knowledge or something one knows
Authentication can be based on something which the person seeking to authenticate himself knows. The obvious examples are a Personal Identification Number (hereinafter: PIN) or passwords.[8] The authentication may serve identification or authorisation purposes. The PIN or password has to be checked against information, such as an Access Control List (hereinafter: ACL)[9] that is held by the server and which evaluates the authentication attempt.

Cryptography: more advanced means of authentication make use of the possibilities that modern cryptography offers. Cryptography is the science of encrypting and decrypting messages. Encryption is the conver-

---

[8] For instance, the Microsoft Password is based on this 'technology'.

[9] An ACL is a list containing the names or other identifiers of the entities that are authorised to use the 'guarded' resource.

sion of the bits from which a message is made up to another form in order to hide the content of the message. The message in its unintelligible form is called a ciphertext. Decryption is the opposite process of converting the ciphertext into plaintext. Modern cryptography makes use of advanced mathematics to perform the aforementioned processes. Encryption involves, apart from the plaintext and the algorithm that performs the encryption (i.e., the cipher), one or more keys. Encryption could also be done without keys, but that would imply that the cipher has to be kept secret. For modern applications this constitutes an unworkable requirement; after all, software that embodies the cipher has to be distributed in order to enable users to encrypt and decrypt. The hopes of keeping a distributed cipher secret are at best very low. Therefore, the encryption that is dealt with in this book involves keys that have to be kept secret, whereas the encryption algorithm is open to the public. With respect to the keys involved in encryption, one can distinguish between symmetric and public key encryption algorithms.

Symmetric encryption
Symmetric encryption algorithms: in a symmetric encryption algorithm the key that is used for decryption can be calculated from the key that is used for encryption or the other way round. Most symmetric encryption algorithms use the same key to both encrypt and decrypt messages. The 'Data Encryption Standard' (DES) is the most well known example of a symmetric encryption algorithm.[10] The use of DES was compulsory for in the U.S. and binding on Federal agencies for the protection of sensitive, unclassified information. In December 2001, the U.S. Department of Commerce announced the successor to DES – the Rijndael algorithm – as the new Advanced Encryption Standard (hereinafter: AES).[11] The new AES will also be compulsory for U.S. federal agencies and is expected to become widely

---

[10] National Bureau of Standards, *Data Encryption Standard*, Springfield (VA): U.S. Department of Commerce/National Technical Information Service 1977 (Federal Information Processing Standards Publication No. 46).

[11] Department of Commerce, National Institute of Standards and Technology, Announcing Approval of Federal Information Processing Standard (FIPS) 197, Advanced Encryption Standard (AES) [Docket No. 000929280-1201-01] RIN 0693-ZA42, Federal Register: 6 December 2001 (Vol. 66, No. 235), Notices, pp. 63369-63371.

used in the private sector as well. S/MIME and TLS – both explained later in this chapter – are examples of 'private' applications of the AES.

Symmetric encryption can be used for authentication purposes or electronic signatures in the following way. If two parties share a key and a symmetric encryption algorithm, they can send encrypted messages to each other. If the receiver decrypts the message with the key he shares with the sender, the plain text becomes visible and under the assumption that the key has been kept secret, the receiver can be sure that the message stems from the sender. If the application of the said key does not yield an intelligible plain text, the message does not originate from the sender or its integrity has become compromised along the way.

This scheme has several drawbacks:

- It is assumed that the receiver can recognise a plaintext as such when he sees it. This may not be self-evident if machine language or other technical information is being sent.
- The scheme does not prevent that the sender can subsequently deny having sent the message by stating that the confidentiality of the key became compromised. Such a denial is called repudiation of origin.
- Key distribution is the Achilles' heel. As described above, every two parties that want to send authenticated messages to each other must share a key that is unknown to all other persons. If a person wants to be able to communicate in an authenticated manner with twenty other people, he must have twenty keys, one shared with every one of the twenty persons. The problem is to get the keys to the parties while the confidentiality of the key remains warranted. For safety reasons, it is furthermore desirable to renew the keys regularly, thus further complicating the key distribution problem.

With respect to the assumption that the receiver can recognise a plaintext as such when he sees it, the following can be said. There is a way to make this assumption superfluous. In order to explain this we have to go back to checksums. As we have seen, the integrity of a message can be checked by means of a checksum, such as a CRC. A CRC is however vulnerable to manipulation; a person who intercepts a message between sender and recipient may not only change the contents of the message, but may also

recalculate the CRC. In such a case, the recipient cannot detect the manipulation with the help of the CRC. In order to prohibit this type of manipulation, checksums have been developed that require a secret key to calculate
their value. The most well known example of such a checksum is the
Message Authentication Code (hereinafter: MAC). Apart from integrity purposes, such keyed checksums can be used for authentication purposes. The
sender sends his message along with the keyed checksum of the message.
The receiver of the message calculates the checksum of the message with
the help of the key. If the newly calculated checksum equals the one that
came along with the message, the message was not changed while in transit. It also stems from the sender, because the checksum was calculated
using the key which the sender and receiver share. If they are not equal the
message was altered after sending or the indicated sender did not send it. In
such a case the receiver knows that he cannot trust the message.

IPsec is an example of an application that makes use of keyed
checksums. In order to counteract IP-spoofing attacks, a keyed checksum
is calculated over a part of the IP-header that includes the indication of
the sender's IP address. Upon the arrival of the packet, the receiver can
check the integrity of (part of) the header. He is thus able to authenticate
on the basis of the sender's IP address indicated in the header, while the
risk of a spoofing attack is suitably reduced.

The second problem concerned repudiation of origin: the sender states
that his key became known to a third person and that the message does
not originate from him. Symmetric encryption as such does not have a solution for this problem. This does not mean that nothing can be done
about this problem. Additional technological measures can be taken. By
using smart cards and biometrics, access to the key can be secured, thus
lessening the credibility of a statement indicating that the confidentiality
has become compromised. This does not, admittedly, provide a watertight
solution.

The problem of key distribution can be alleviated in various ways:

• All messages are sent via a mutually trusted third party (hereinafter:
  TTP).[12]

---

[12] Schneier 1996, pp. 35-37.

- The keys are distributed using symmetric encryption itself.[13]
- The keys are distributed using asymmetric encryption. This will be dealt with later in the context of Secure Socket Layers and TLS.

Here, the two former options are dealt with. The first option concerns the situation in which all messages are sent via a TTP. In this case, everybody shares a key with the TTP. Thus, the trusted third party shares, for example, a key with a party, called Alice, and another key with a party, called Bob. If Alice wants to send Bob a message, she sends it to the trusted third party, encrypted with the key she shares with the TTP. The trusted third party receives the message and knows that it stems from Alice as it is encrypted with the key which Alice and the trusted third party share. The trusted third party decrypts the message and adds a certificate, stating that the accompanying message stems from Alice; next he encrypts the message and certificate together with the key he shares with Bob and sends it to Bob. The encrypted message as encrypted by Alice will be stored in the trusted third party's database, or it will be sent to Bob together with the message. Upon reception, Bob knows that the message originates from Alice, because of the certificate added by the trusted third party. He also knows that it has come directly from the trusted third party because of the key used. The authenticity may also afterwards be proved towards a third party as the trusted third party retains the message as encrypted by Alice (or gets it back from Bob) and can issue a certificate as to the origin of the message to the third party.

Bob may afterwards try to reuse Alice's message by changing the message into one that suits his purposes better or by stating that the certificate belongs to another message altogether, but he will not be able to prove 'signing by Alice'. After all, if the message he claims to be certified by the trusted third party is encrypted with Alice's key, the result will be different from the original message as encrypted with Alice's key. Thus, the trusted third party is able to denounce Bob.

The key distribution problem is alleviated in that everybody only needs to have one key, viz., the key he shares with the TTP, assuming that there is only one TTP. This authentication scheme nevertheless dem-

---

[13] Ford and Baum 1997, pp. 120-122.

onstrates some drawbacks. As all the messages have to pass through the 'hands' of the trusted third party, it may become a bottleneck perform-ancewise. Perhaps more importantly, the trusted third party holds a data-base that contains all the keys, because everybody shares a key with the trusted third party. If its key database becomes compromised, the entire authentication scheme would become useless in one stroke. An advantage of this approach could however be that it is easy to incorporate other TTP services, such as timestamping and limited non-repudiation of origin.[14]

The second option concerns the situation that symmetric encryption it-self is used to distribute keys. The ANSI X9.17 standard provides an ex-ample of this idea.

The standard distinguishes three types of keys: master keys, key-en-crypting keys and session keys. Session keys are used to protect the data that actually need to be authenticated. Key-encrypting keys are used to communicate session keys. Master keys are distributed in a safe way, off-line. These are long-term keys used between two systems and used to en-crypt key-encrypting and session keys.

An authentication scheme can be set up with a key centre. Every com-municating system shares a master key with the key centre. If a system wants to communicate with another system, it asks the key centre to send a (key-encrypting) key to both itself and the other system. Since the key centre shares master keys with both systems, it is able to do so in a confi-dential way. Both systems now share a key, viz., the key-encrypting key. With the help of this key, they can communicate directly or they can use the key to negotiate a session key with which they can then communicate. Whichever of the two keys they use, the receiving system can be sure that the message received stems from the other system. Admittedly, this does not hold true if the key becomes compromised, if the sender untruthfully states that the key has become compromised, or if the key centre plays foul. Nonetheless, the key distribution problem is alleviated. The number of master keys that have to be distributed manually is equal to the number of participating systems. Admittedly, also the master keys have to be re-newed now and then, but the frequency with which this has to be done is rather low. A great advantage of the system is that the session keys and

---

[14] I speak here of limited non-repudiation of origin, because the problem with a claimed loss of the secrecy of the key can of course not be undone by a TTP.

the key-encrypting keys can be renewed frequently, thus complicating attempts to break the encryption.

Both described alleviations to the key distribution problem do require that the key distribution takes place in a confidential way, thus complicating key distribution. Public key encryption addresses this drawback, as will be explained hereinafter.

2.4 PUBLIC KEY ENCRYPTION

2.4.1 Public key encryption in general

In the case of symmetric encryption both parties to a communication share a secret, visually the key. Public key encryption makes use of two keys: a private and a public key. These keys are different and the one cannot be calculated from the other, at least not in a reasonable period of time. The private key is to be kept private. Only the owner of the key knows the private key. The public key on the other hand, can be made public, for instance through a directory service on the Internet or it can be sent to somebody who might need it. Well-known examples of public key encryption are RSA, DSS, and DSA. From a user perspective they function in a comparable way:

If a message is encrypted with the public key it can only be decrypted with the associated private key. For RSA also the opposite holds true: once encrypted with a private key it can only be decrypted, using the associated public key.

In order to safeguard the confidentiality of a message during transport the sender encrypts the message using the public key of the intended recipient. If the recipient has indeed kept his private key secret, he is the only one that is able to decipher the message, as he is the only person that has the associated private key at his disposal. Any eavesdropper along the line only sees a ciphertext he cannot understand, nor decrypt. The confidentiality is guaranteed.

There is however one drawback. Encrypting an entire message with a public key is computationally expensive; thus it may take a while for a computer to calculate the encryption. Therefore, in practice messages are usually encrypted using symmetric encryption. The key needed for symmetric encryption is generated by one of the parties to the communication and this so-called session key is sent to the other party, encrypted with the other party's public key. In this way, one makes use of the fact that a session key is often much smaller than the message that is encrypted with it. The public key encryption will thus take less time. The session key can be exchanged before the actual message is sent (as is the case with a Secure Socket Layer as we will see) or it can be sent together with the encrypted message.[15]

Apart from the purpose of confidentiality, public key cryptography can be used to guarantee the integrity and authenticity of a message. A simple way to achieve this is the following. Alice wants to send Bob a message. Alice encrypts the message using her private key and sends it to Bob. Bob deciphers it using Alice's public key. If there appears a message that makes sense to Bob, the message must have been encrypted with Alice's private key, and must thus stem from Alice and still be intact. If the encryption only yields abracadabra, something along the transmission path has gone wrong (e.g., somebody has tampered with the message) or the message stems from somebody impersonating Alice.

However, there are disadvantages to this approach. The difference between messages that make sense and abracadabra might be subjective. But that is maybe not the most important drawback. Encryption by means of a private key is computationally expensive. Therefore, encrypting the message in its entirety may cost a lot of time. It would be easier if only a smaller string needed encryption. Well, there is a way to do this, namely by using a hash function.

In order to understand this, it has to be explained what a hash function is. A hash function takes a variable length input string – for instance a message – and returns a fixed length output string, called the hash value. The idea is that if even one bit is changed in the input string, the hash value also will change.[16] A hash function can be used to determine with a reasonable degree of assurance whether two strings are equal, without comparing the strings themselves. A hash value is sometimes called a digest. In cryptography, a special type of hash function is important: the

---

[15] See Schneier 1996, p. 50.

[16] Mathematically this statement may not be provable, but generally it is held that a hash function gives a reasonable assurance of accuracy. See Schneier 1996, p. 30.

one-way hash function. With a one-way hash function it is easy to com-
pute the hash value from a given input string, but is very hard – in practical terms impossible – to calculate the original input string from the hash
value. SHA-1 is a much-used hashing algorithm.[17]

The authenticity and integrity of a message may be verified using public key cryptography and one-way hashing functions. It works like this.
Suppose that Alice wants to send Bob a message. Alice and Bob have
agreed in advance upon an encryption algorithm – let us say RSA – and a
hash function. Alice writes her message and calculates the hash value of
the completed message. This hash value she encrypts with her private
key. The encrypted hash is called a digital signature. Finally, she sends
the message and the digital signature to Bob. Having received the message and the digital signature, Bob does two things. He calculates the
hash value from the message and he decrypts the digital signature using
Alice's public key. If nothing untoward has happened during the transmission (nobody has tampered with the message), these two values are
equal and the digital signature is valid. This can be explained as follows.
The deciphering of the digital signature yields the hash value, as calculated by Alice. If this value is equal to the hash value, newly calculated
by Bob, the message was not altered between the moment Alice calculated the value and the moment Bob calculated it, i.e., not altered during
the transmission. At the same time, it is clear that the message stems from
Alice, as she is the only person who possesses her private key. Thus, she
is the only person who could have encrypted the hash value in such a way
that deciphering the value with her public key would yield the message's
hash value. If a hacker altered the message while in transit, the two values would not be equal. If the hacker maintained Alice's digital signature,
the deciphered digital signature – i.e., the hash value of the original message – would not equal the hash value of the altered message. After all, it
is a property of a hash function that two different inputs yield, with a
large degree of certainty, two different outcomes, i.e., hash values. If the
hacker would want to add a new digital signature, he would run into the
problem that he does not know Alice's private key. So he cannot produce
a digital signature that reflects the new hash value.

---

[17] See FIPS PUBC 180-1: Secure Hash Standard, 17 April 1995, National Institute of
Standards and Technology.

Instead of speaking of encryption with a private key and decryption with a public key, I will henceforth refer to these processes as signing (with the help of one's private key) and verifying (with the help of the sender's public key) respectively. As there are many different algorithms for signing (other than RSA mentioned earlier), speaking of encryption and decryption is not always correct.

2.4.2   Certification

Public Key Distribution
Distribution of public keys can take one of several forms. A party to a communication might send its public key to the other party. It is also possible that there is some public file or directory in which public keys and identifying (or authorising) information are stored. A public key crypto system has the advantage over a symmetric encryption system that its key distribution is much simpler. The 'other' party only needs to know the public key and this key can easily be distributed, because it is 'public'. There is no harm in the reception of the key by persons other than the intended recipient of the signed message. The key may even be broadcast over the network.

Nevertheless, there is a problem. How do I know that a public key that is presented to me as Alice's public key is indeed *her* public key? It might as well be the public key of somebody impersonating Alice. In a computer network I cannot easily verify that it really is Alice's public key. However, it seems not to be an insurmountable problem and there are ways to solve this problem. These solutions will be dealt with in the following section(s).

Verification of Public Keys
In the previous section it was explained that it is not easy to verify that a public key really belongs to the person that is claimed to be its 'owner'. In order to overcome this difficulty, Loren M. Kohnfelder introduced in 1978 in his bachelor thesis the notion of a certificate.[18] A certificate as Kohnfelder views it contains a name and key information pair and is signed by the

---

[18] L.M. Kohnfelder, Toward a Reliable Public Key Cryptosystem, Bachelor's thesis, MIT Department of Electrical Engineering, <http://thesis.mit.edu:80/>, accessed in 2001.

'Public File'. The 'Public File' is a central authority that is trusted by all communicants. It is the only entity that can create and modify certificates, all communicants can read the certificates of the Public File and the Public File only creates certificates with names and associated keys.

Later, the term certificate was generally used for a wider notion than Kohnfelder had envisaged in 1978. The use of the word certificate has since then been widened in several respects. In the first place a certificate would not just contain a name, but instead any identifying information could be in a certificate. Sometimes a certificate does not even contain identifying information, but instead holds an authorisation, as is the case with SPKI. Also combinations of identifying information and authorisations are possible, e.g., in SPKI/SDSI. In the second place the issuer of the certificate does not have to be a trusted central authority, but could be anybody (for instance, in the case of a PGP web of trust). Therefore, I understand that a certificate is a binding between a public key and identifying information or an authorisation, a binding which is confirmed by the signature of the certifier, often a trusted third party.

A certificate might or might not be issued at the request of the person whose public key is to be certified. The party issuing the certificate is called the Certification Authority (hereinafter: the CA). A CA will generally only issue a certificate if it has satisfied itself that the information contained therein is correct. The task of verifying information that is to be included in a certificate is performed by a so-called Registering Authority (hereinafter: RA). What data a certificate contains, which checks take place, what the exact meaning of the certified information is, are all questions that might be answered differently by different CAs. Even a single CA may have more than one policy concerning these issues, dependent upon the application for which the certificate and signature is required.

If somebody wants to send me an authenticated message, he may sign it with his digital signature and send a certificate of his public key along with it. The certificate not only gives me his public key, but he also enables me to verify that it really is his public key, because the certificate is signed by the CA. Saying this, I assume that I have the CA's public key and that I trust it for the concerned certification. If, however, I do not have the public key of the CA or if I do not know whether I want to trust the CA, another solution is in order as will be seen in the next section.

Why do you trust a CA?

Somebody might send me a certificate of his digital signature, signed by a CA. This CA may be a CA who I trust, whose signature I can verify and whose policy I approve of. In this case there is of course no problem. However, if I do not know the CA and do not know whether I can trust him, some solution has to found. The simplest solution in this case would be if a CA that I trust and whose public key I have could vouch for the unknown CA, i.e., if the trusted CA could provide a certificate of the digital signature of the unknown CA. If such a trusted CA exists, I might want to trust the unknown CA. But what if such a trusted CA cannot be found? Then I could try to find an intermediate CA that can vouch for the unknown CA and whose digital signature is vouched for by a CA that I trust. If I can find such a CA, I might want to trust the certificate for which it all began. If such an intermediate CA does not exist, a solution has to be found. But the solution might – by now – have become a little predictable: try to find a second intermediary CA so that a chain of CAs comes to exist, beginning with the CA that I trust and ending in the CA that certifies the public key I want to use, such that each CA in the chain can vouch for its successor in the chain; the last CA certifies the public key I need to be sure about in order to verify the digital signature. A system of chained CAs is generally called a Public Key Infrastructure (hereinafter: PKI). A PKI is sometimes also referred to as a trust hierarchy.

There are however a few drawbacks to this idea.

- There might not exist a chain from a trusted CA to the untrusted CA. If this is the case, a relying party might choose to trust an untrusted CA. Perhaps he has means outside the PKI to gather information about the unknown CA that might increase trust in the CA.
- It might be time-consuming to find a chain.
- The chain is only as strong as its weakest link. Therefore, the longer the chain becomes, the greater the risk that a CA in the chain has become compromised. A compromised CA could vouch for untrustworthy other CAs and thus all successors of a compromised CA might be untrustworthy.
- Hitherto, I have spoken of vouching for a CA and vouching for a digital signature as if this were a simple, unambiguous activity. Of

course, it is not. A CA might receive somebody's digital signature and accompanying (identifying) data through various more or less secure ways. The checks and verification of the signature/data offered, might take place for a particular – low or high profile – purpose. The verification of data might be more or less thoroughly performed. Perhaps the checks and verifications are not up to my standards. If I look at it in this way, there might also exist weakest links, not in the sense of compromised CAs, but in the sense that there is a CA in the chain who vouches for public keys in a way that is not up to my standards or is unsuitable for my purposes.

Hereinafter, I will mention a number of ways to address these drawbacks. However, it must be borne in mind that an approach might take away or reduce one drawback at the expense of another or by introducing a new drawback.

- A hierarchical structure of CAs: A hierarchy could take several forms. Let us have a look at a hierarchy in which there is one root common to all users of the PKI, i.e., the top of the hierarchy. Let us suppose that all CAs in the hierarchy vouch for CAs that are below them in that hierarchy. Such a hierarchical structure might bring about several advantages. If one trusts a CA high in the hierarchy, then there exists a path to every CA in the sub-tree below the trusted CA. If one trusts the root, there exists a path to every CA in the hierarchy. The paths may be relatively short thus reducing the risks associated with larger paths.[19] A drawback might be that the root, because of its central position, is a very interesting object of attack. Once compromised, it might become a viable basis for misuse.
- Multiple disjunctive paths and specifying a maximum length of certification paths. If one wants to reduce the risk of compromised links in chains, one could demand that there be found not one, but a number of paths from a given untrusted CA to a trusted CA. If those chains have no 'intermediate links' in common, the risk associated with compromised links diminishes. A drawback is that multiple chains

---

[19] I assume that the hierarchy is 'balanced'.

might not exist, or it may take a long time to find them. Another way to enhance security is to trust chains only up to a certain length. The consequence may be that sometimes no chain can be found that is sufficiently short.

- Transparency of policies and freedom to choose which CAs to trust. Above it was identified as a problem that the certifications of a CA might not be up to your standard or not suitable for the purpose for which you want to use them. Transparency concerning a policy used by a CA enables you to determine whether you want to trust a CA or not. The software you use must enable you to specify which CAs you trust and for what purposes you trust them. Browser software sometimes has by default set some CAs as trusted CAs. This might not conform to your demands. Sometimes it is not possible to differentiate between CAs with respect to the purposes for which you trust them.[20]

- Certificate policy and CPS: every CA within a PKI adheres to the same certificate policy or to the same certification practise statement (hereinafter: CPS). For interoperability sake it may be desirable to have certifications between different PKIs, but this is a very complicated matter. As CAs from different PKIs, might employ different procedures and practices for different purposes, it may be difficult to establish certification between PKIs without compromising security, auditability and liability.

- A closed environment: if a PKI is embedded in an organisational structure there might be means (outside the PKI) by which the policies and functioning of CAs can be controlled.

PKI

There are different ideas about how trust in a CA is brought about. Different ideas about trust are reflected in the structure of a PKI. Here, two approaches are being dealt with. First PGPs web of trust is discussed. It focuses primarily on the relying party and his means of expressing trust in a certifying

---

[20] For instance Internet Explorer 5.0 has the option to set the purposes for which you trust CAs. But once you have specified that you trust a CA for purpose X, then all the CAs in your list of trusted CAs are trusted for purpose X. There is only one setting for all CAs.

party. Secondly, a model is dealt with that focuses much more on the CA and the practices and procedures he employs.

PGP's web of trust
In PGP there are no formal CAs organised in hierarchies. Instead any PGP user can sign identification-public key bindings and thus 'certify' public keys. If I have somebody's public key and I trust this person to act as a 'trusted introducer' I might instruct my PGP software to accept 'certificates' from this person. So by considering him to be a trusted introducer, I can not only safely communicate with him, but also with the persons from whom he has a reliable public key. As this person might in turn accept a third person as a trusted introducer, I might also accept certificates about the persons this third person trusts. Of course this may be continued with following persons. On the other hand, somebody who has my public key and considers me to be a trusted introducer, might issue a certificate with my identity and public key. Through this mechanism, in an informal way, a circle of persons may be created with whom I might safely communicate and who may safely communicate with me. In PGP terminology, there is a web of trust. However, because this is all done rather informally, there are limitations to the trust that can be placed in certificates. Therefore, PGP provides a relying party with a means to differentiate between certificates according to the trust he places in them. A user holds a local file, called a key ring. In this key ring, a user stores information about the public keys he holds. Apart from the key itself, it is stored whether the user considers the public key to be a valid key. In the second place the user stores in the keying to what extent he trusts the 'owner' of the public key to certify other public keys. There are several options. Of course, he can indicate that he never trusts the key for certification purposes, in which case certificates signed with this key are never used. He can indicate that he does not know whether the key can be trusted. In that case, PGP will always ask the user whether the key can be trusted when verifying the signature under a certificate. Furthermore, he can indicate that he marginally trusts a public key. In that case a certificate signed with the corresponding private key will not be trusted, unless PGP can find another 'marginal' certificate for the same key. In that case, the key-user binding that is certified by two marginal certificates is trusted. Optionally, one can set the number of marginal certifiers required for trusting a public key higher than two. Finally, a relying party might

indicate that it always trusts a public key, for both signing and certification purposes. PGP is very much oriented towards the relying party, giving him the freedom to make decisions himself about the trust that is to be placed in certificates.

However, for reasons of limited accountability PGP is less suitable for professional purposes.

'CA-centric approach'
Trust in CAs can of course be based on the fact that they are professional entities that perform their function according to a published 'Certification Practise Statement' (CPS). The American Bar Association Digital Signature Guidelines 1996 define a CPS as 'a statement of the practises which a certification authority employs in issuing certificates'.[21] Subjects that may be covered by a CPS include: certification request, verifications of identifying and authorisation-information to be performed at enrolment, the issuing of certificates, certificate classes (i.e., the different service levels provided by the CA), suspension and revocation of certificates, the technology to be used and legal issues, such as, warranties, limitation of liability and procedural provisions. PKIs based on X.509 v.3 certificates and Privacy Enhanced Mail (hereinafter: PEM) provide examples of this approach to trust in CAs. In order to enhance certification between CAs, it is desirable that all CAs within a PKI conform themselves to the same CPS. Certification between CAs that have different CPSs, practices, procedures and technologies are very complicated. Inter-CA certification might even prove to be unfeasible; the meaning of a certification might become ambiguous. Some well-known providers of certification services are VeriSign, RSA Security and KPN (the main Dutch telecom operator).

The format of certificates
In the course of time many certificate formats have been defined. X.509 v.3 certificates and SPKI will be dealt with here.

X.509 v.3 certificates
X.509 is an ITU-T Recommendation that has become a de facto standard.

---

[21] See <http://www.abanet.org/ftp/pub/scitech/ds-ms.doc>, accessed in 2001.

The third version of X.509 was introduced in 1996 and has become a widely used format for certificates. A X.509 certificate contains the following fields:

Version
This field indicates the version of the certificate format (X.509) that is being used.

Certificate Serial Number
The CA assigns a Serial Number to each certificate it issues. If the certificate is to be revoked, the CRL (see hereinafter) will be able to specify the certificate by its Serial Number.

Signature Algorithm Identifier
This identifies the algorithm which the certificate issuer uses for his signature.

Issuer Name
The X.500 name of the entity that issued the certificate.

Validity Period
A certificate is only valid for a certain period of time. The Validity Period is specified by giving its begin date and time and its end date and time. If a certificate is not prematurely revoked it can be used up until the end of the Validity Period.

Subject Name
This is the name of the subject whose public key is being certified. The format of this name conforms to the X.500 standard. It is called a Distinguished Name and it is supposed to be globally unique.

Subject Public Key Information
This field contains the value of the subject's public key and an identification of the algorithm the key is to be used with.

Optionally a version 3 certificate may contain the fields 'Issuer Unique Identifier' and 'Subject Unique Identifier'. These fields are added because for some applications that have to handle certificates X.500 names are meaningless; the added fields can be filled with data than can be handled by those systems. Finally, X.509 allows for user definable extensions. ISO/ IEC, ITU and ANSI X9 have developed a number of standard extensions to X.509. Here a few of these extensions are dealt with. One such extension is the field 'Key Usage'; in this field the purposes for which the certified key may be used can be indicated. Examples of such purposes are, *inter alia*: digital signature, non-repudiation and CRL-signing. This field may additionally be flagged as critical or non-critical. If it is flagged critical a user relying on the certificate for purposes that fall outside the CAs policy as indicated in the Key Usage field acts at his own risk. Another standard extension is called 'Certificate Policies'. This field contains – unsurprisingly – a reference to a Certificate Policy. Certificate Policies are statements that may be drawn up in addition to a CPS and that may partially cover the same subjects as a CPS. A CA may define several certificate policies, some low quality certificate policies and other higher quality certificate policies. One might for instance define a 'General Practise' policy for casual e-mail messages and higher quality 'Financial Transactions' policy for transactions exceeding a certain Euro value, e.g., Euro 1000. The user of a certificate may then program his system to accept only certificates that have been handled according to a certain quality level by indicating what certificate policies he is willing to accept. I finally mention the field 'Policy Mappings' that contains information about the equivalence of certificate policies defined by different CAs.

Attribute Certificates
Information that is contained in certificate-extensions can be issued by a CA. Sometimes, it is however not obvious to have the CA issue certain information. He might for instance not be the right person to issue authorisation information. For this reason attribute certificates have been devised. They are separate certificates that contain additional information and are associated with a signature certificate. X9.57 is a well-known definition of an attribute certificate that was originated by the American Bankers Association (ABA) and adopted by ANSI. Attribute Certificates may be handled by a separate Authority: an Attribute Authority (hereinafter: AA).

Simple Public Key Infrastructure
X.509 certificates may become very complex, as we have seen above. SPKI[22] is an attempt to construct a simpler certification scheme, doing away with unnecessary ballast of X.509. SPKI certificates are authorisation certificates, as opposed to identity certificates.[23] This means that an authorisation (e.g., to have access to a certain computer system) is directly associated with a key. It functions as follows. The 'guard' of a 'resource' receives a request to use the resource. This request is signed with a digital signature and accompanied by an authorisation certificate. The guard verifies the signature, but does not learn the identity of the key holder, as the certificate does not contain the name (or other identifying information) of the key holder. The certificate just contains the public key and the authorisation. This brings about an important privacy advantage to the requestor, as his identity will not be revealed to the guard.[24]

For the sake of completeness, I mention that it is possible to associate an attribute certificate (which may contain a name or other identifying information) to an SPKI certificate. Such attribute certificates are issued by an AA. This can of course be another entity than the CA that certifies the SPKI certificate.

Simple Key Management for Internet Protocols (SKIP)
It provides for safe IP transport. It does not build on the establishment of a session, but provides for authentication and privacy on the network layer, even if this uses a sessionless datagram protocol.

Revocation of a certificate
A certificate has a validity period. Typically, a validity period may range from several months to a number of years. In principle the certificate is valid during this period. However, it may happen that there is a reason to withdraw the certificate before its validity period comes to an end. This may be necessary if the private key that corresponds to the certified public key has been compromised, or, e.g., if other certified data have become

---

[22] <http://www.ietf.org/html.charters/spki-charter.html>, accessed in 2001.
[23] <ftp://ftp.isi.edu/in-notes/rfc2693.txt>, accessed in 2001.
[24] See Ellison 1997.

obsolete. A CA may at the request of the 'subject' of a certificate or without request revoke a certificate. A CA revokes a certificate by placing it on a Certificate Revocation List (hereinafter: a CRL), published by him. The CA signs the CRL with his digital signature, so as to assure its authenticity and integrity. It has a timestamp ingrained in it, so as to assure its publication time. A CA can choose to publish CRLs at scheduled points in time, for instance every day at 12:00 pm or every week on Wednesday. This might mean that some time passes before a certificate, known to be no longer valid, will appear in a CRL. There is, however, a good reason to do so. Because CRLs are published at moments that are known in advance, it is always clear what the latest CRL is. If a CA would publish a CRL off cycle, there is no assurance that the persons for whom it is meant will see it. Moreover, a hacker could try to remove such a CRL from the server or frustrate its transportation, without the persons relying on certificates and CRLs noticing it. They would consider the predecessing CRL to be the latest CRL. Another solution would be to use secure servers and secure transmissions, but it is questionable whether a server could ever be reliably safe.

Examples of Dutch PKIs
Several companies and organisations are offering TTP services in the Netherlands. Here a brief indication of the activities of some of them is given.

PKI Overheid
On 17 December 1999, the Dutch Cabinet decided to install the PKI Overheid Taskforce.[25] The aim of the project is to attain an infrastructure for reliable and confidential communication. This infrastructure serves three domains: communication between government institutions, communication between government institutions and companies and communication between government institutions and the public at large. The milestones to date are the completion of the specification of requirements in 2002[26] and the establishment in December 2002 of the root certificates of the entire PKI and of the

---

[25] Kamerstukken (Parliamentary Documents) II, 1999/2000, 26387, No. 5 (Letter from the Minister for Urban Policy and Integration of Ethnic Minorities).
[26] See <http://www.pkioverheid.nl/>, accessed in 2003.

three domains.[27] Certificates – in their terminology including private keys – are placed on smartcards.

DigiNotar
DigiNotar is a TTP that came about through co-operation between civil law notaries and IT specialists. The notaries function as RAs and the central organisation DigiNotar BV as a CA. The services of DigiNotar comprise a wide area. Accordingly,
Its CPS discerns several types of certificates. In order to give an indication, they are here concisely described by indicating who or what they identify and what authorisations they contain.[28] A natural person certificate (Natuurlijk Persoonscertificaat) identifies a natural person. A company certificate (Bedrijfscertificaat) identifies a person authorised to represent the company. A personal organisation certificate (Persoonsgebonden Organisatiecertificaat) identifies a natural person as an employee of an organisation without indicating any authority to represent the organisation. A professional certificate (Beroepscertificaat) identifies a natural person as a self-employed professional.[29] An envelope certificate (Envelopcertificaat) identifies an organisation or a department of an organisation without identifying a natural person. A relation certificate (Relatiecertificaat) is a certificate that identifies a 'relation' of a DigiNotar client. The client himself verifies the identity of the relation at the personalisation phase. The certificate is to be used in a limited circle only. An SSL server certificate identifies the domain name or the IP address of a server. A signing server certificate identifies a department or organisation as the user of a server. Applications running on the server can make use of this certificate. A software signing certificate is used to electronically sign software. The

---

[27] S. van der Schaaf, Beveiligd Verkeer Nederland. Omvangrijke implementatie van digitale certificaten rijksoverheid nog ver weg, *Computable* 13 March 2003, see <http://www.computable.nl/>.

[28] CPS DigiNotar 2 May 2003, Handleiding en algemene voorwaarden bij de verkrijging en het gebruik van DigiNotar Certificate Services, versie 3.0, <http://www.diginotar.nl/CPSconceptv3.0.pdf>. This CPS was still a concept at the time of writing.

[29] Apart from a professional certificate, a deputy professional certificate (Beroepscertificaat Waarnemer) can be issued. It identifies a natural person as a substitute for a self-employed professional.

organisation or department that makes the software available can thus be identified. Apart from the above, a custom-made certificate can be issued.

Under the name DigiOverheid, certificates are issued that conform to PKI Overheid.

DigiNotar also performs timestamping services. Escrow services are being developed.

DigiNotar will try to obtain accreditation as a Certification Service Provider (hereinafter: CSP) as meant in Article 18.16 Dutch Telecommunications Act (which is the implementation of Article 3.2 Directive 1999/93/EC); accreditation signals comply with ETSI Standard TS 101456.

Enschede-Sdu

Traditionally, Enschede-Sdu prints Dutch Passports. It now performs a number of TTP services. For the purpose of this book, the following can be mentioned: it functions as a CA, it has RA services in that it has a central card management system with a provision for secured and authorised card management at a distance (i.e., at a RA station). Enschede-Sdu performs key management services, consisting of the generation, loading, distribution and (optionally) archiving of cryptographic key material. It has directory services, consisting of the publication and/or distribution of certificates and CRLs via the Internet, ISDN and private networks. It performs code-signing services, with respect to JAVA and C-Code. It takes care of electronic and graphic personalisation of electronic ID cards. As a CSP, Enschede-Sdu intends to complete the certification scheme of TTP.NL, thus determining that it conforms to ETSI Standard TS 101456. Enschede-Sdu can also issue certificates that comply with the requirements of PKI Overheid.

Other TTPs in the Netherlands include KPN Entercom Solutions, PinkRoccade Megaplex (ETSI certified)[30] and Ubizen.

---

[30] See <https://www.pki.pinkroccade.com/>, accessed in 2003.

2.4.3 PKI based authentication mechanisms

XML Digital Signatures
The Extensible Markup Language (hereinafter: XML) is a markup language for creating structured documents that can be used over the web.[31] XML documents can easily be transferred between applications and organisations without compromising their interpretation and validation. Furthermore, XML is very flexible, in that it allows for the creation of one's own markup tags. The definition of these markup tags can be laid down in a Document Type Declaration (DTD), enabling easy validation and interpretation of documents created according to the self-designed format.

The IETF and W3C established a working group in 1999 which aims to produce a datamodel, syntax and processing for attaching a digital signature to digital content and in particular to XML content. In April 2001 the working group released its second W3C Candidate Recommendation on XML-Signature syntax and processing,[32] which is its most recent result at the moment of writing this text.

XML Digital Signatures are not a new technology for encryption or hashing. It merely provides a structure for the composition and processing of signatures, thus enabling the use of existing or future digital signature technology to its fullest potential. In order to clarify the XML Digital Signatures, its functioning and operation will here be explained in some detail. According to the Recommendation, an XML digital signature is an XML document with a format as shown in Figure 2.

The XML digital signature comprises, at most, four elements: SignedInfo, SignatureValue, KeyInfo and Object (which is optional).

SignedInfo is a composed element. It may optionally contain the element CanonicalisationMethod. In order to understand the meaning of this element, it is first explained what canonicalisation is. Text files, including XML files, may use different representation conventions for, for instance, character encoding and line termination. Different representations do not change the text to the eye of the human beholder, but the underlying en-

---

[31] XML is actually a scaled-down version of SGML which is too complicated for straightforward use over the web.

[32] See <http://www.w3.org/TR/2001/CR-xmldsig-core-20010419/>, accessed in 2001.

```
<Signature>

     <SignedInfo>
          (CanonicalizationMethod)
          (SignatureMethod)
          (<Reference (URI=)? >
               (Transforms)?
               (DigestMethod)
               (DigestValue)
          </Reference>)+
     </SignedInfo>

     (SignatureValue)

     (KeyInfo)?

     (Object)*

</Signature>
```

Figure 2
An XML document showing an XML digital signature.

coding in the file may be different. Often text files are automatically adapted when entering a system or being processed by an application that uses representation conventions other than those employed in the text file. This might cause problems when verifying a digital signature of a text file that was signed on a system other than the system where the verification takes place. Therefore, for signing and verifying digital signatures one agreed upon representation is used: the so-called canonical form. Before signing a text, it is first 'translated' into canonical form; after that, the hash is calculated over the string of bits that, if seen as a text file, is in canonical form. Subsequently the normal steps in signing a document are taken. For the verification of a signature, the text is first brought into canonical form, before the usual steps for verification are taken. Thus, the different treatments that are encountered when entering a text file in different systems are of no consequence for the verifiability of a signature. In an XML digital signature, the element CanonicalisationMethod is used to communicate what method for canonicalisation is being used. The element Signaturemethod conveys information on the cryptographic functions used for signature and verification and the hash function or MAC. The reference element contains meta-information about the object that is signed. As the reference element may appear more than once in an XML Digital Signature, it is possible to sign more than one information object with a single XML Digital Signature. The reference element may optionally contain an URI to identify the object that has been signed. If it does not contain such an URI it must be clear from the context in which the signature is used what object is being signed.[33] Sometimes a signer performs transformations to the object that is to be signed. The transformations that were executed before calculating the digest can be listed in the 'transform' element. The elements 'DigestMethod' and 'DigestValue' are self-explanatory; the former specifies the method used for calculating the digest, the latter contains the value resulting from calculating the digest over the referenced object.

The SignatureValue is the actual digital signature, calculated over all the information contained in SignedInfo. Keyinfo is an optional element.

---

[33] The object may also be referenced in the optional 'object' element, in which case the reference falls 'outside' the signature.

It may contain information on how the signature can be verified, such as information on how to obtain the public key. In case of a so-called enveloping signature the 'Object' element contains the object being signed. This element is however optional; alternatively the signed object can be referenced in the 'Reference' element that is part of 'SignedInfo'.

XML Signatures form the basis for AuthXML, a standard for exchanging authentication and authorisation information in XML. It also plays a role in the

Security Services Markup Language (hereinafter: S2ML). S2ML is a protocol for exchanging security information, such as authentications and authorisations between partner companies. *Inter alia*, it has been developed to allow visitors to a company's web site to travel to a partner web site without having to re-identify themselves or to request authorisation.

Secure Socket Layer

SSL is an open, non-proprietary protocol, designed by Netscape.[34] It has been approved by the IETF as a standard. The HTTPS protocol is its predecessor; HTTPS will not be dealt with here. The purpose of SSL is to provide confidentiality and integrity with respect to data that are being transferred between servers and clients in open environments. It can also provide for the authentication of the server and eventually of the client involved in communication.

Technically it is an intermediate layer within the Internet architecture, above IP/TCP and below application levels such as http (i.e., the www), IMAP (i.e., e-mail), etc. This means that SSL is available to all applications that might need its services.

How it is done

SSL sets up a session (also known as a connection) between a server and a client that wish to communicate. The session starts with a handshake (an exchange of messages). During the handshake, the server and possibly the client are authenticated and a session key is generated. This is done using public key encryption. Once the handshake has been completed messages

---

[34] Secured Transmission (SSL, HTTPS), <http://www.wdvl.com/Authoring/Tools/Tutorial/secure.html> (accessed in 2001).

that are being exchanged during the session are encrypted using symmetric encryption. Encrypting, decrypting and tamper detection are more efficient using symmetric encryption.

Authentication of the server takes place on the basis of a 'server certificate' which enables the client to perform a verification. Whether verification of the public key of the server is possible depends on the client and the server sharing a CA that they both trust. Mostly, servers have several certificates issued by more than one CA and clients have a list containing several CAs that they trust. Usually, server and client do have at least one CA in common that they both trust, so that verification is possible. A server certificate may contain a name and address of the certificate holder. The client, more specifically the 'web surfer' or 'on-line consumer', is able to view the certificate in his browser. The certificate also holds the domain name of the server for which the certificate is issued. During the handshake, the domain name in the certificate is automatically checked against the one of the server that is participating in the session. If the domain names do not match the authentication fails. This verification is officially not part of the SSL protocol, but is incorporated in the SSL software.

SSL authenticates a server. This means that the connection 'authentically' originates from a server with a certain domain name and is managed by a certain person or other entity. It does not authenticate the documents sent over the connection, other than that the documents stem from the authenticated server. This becomes evident when a third party tampers with the data in the server before they enter the authenticated connection. The data come from an authenticated source, but are not in accordance with what this source would want. Therefore, the level of security applied to the authenticated server remains important.

Verisign is one of the largest Certificate Authorities, issuing SSL server certificates.[35]

Transport Layer Security (TLS)
TLS is the successor to SSL. It is described in RFC 2246. It functions on top of a reliable transport layer such as TCP. It is application protocol inde-

---

[35] See <http://www.verisign.com> , accessed in 2001.

pendent. The functioning of TLS is from a superficial perspective very akin to SSL. Two peers that wish to communicate can be authenticated by TLS. The data they exchange are confidential and their integrity is checked. In order to accomplish these goals, TLS defines a so-called Handshake Protocol and a Record Protocol. By performing the Handshake Protocol, two peers that wish to communicate can be authenticated and an encryption algorithm and a mutually shared encryption key can be negotiated. The 'handshake' is performed using asymmetric encryption. Its function is to set up a secure connection. This connection is governed by the Record Protocol. The data sent during the secure connection can be encrypted using symmetric encryption, the master keys of which are exchanged during the handshake. Despite the similarities, SSL version 3.0 and TLS version 1.0 are not fully interoperable.[36]

Wireless Transport Layer Security protocol (hereinafter: WTLS) is an adaptation of TLS version 1.0 that has been conceived to take into account the special characteristics of the wireless environment, such as low bandwidth, low processing and memory capacity.

Secure Electronic Transactions (SET)
SET is a technical standard for safeguarding payment card purchases made over open networks.[37] It has been developed by Visa and MasterCard with the participation of leading technology companies, such as Microsoft, IBM, Netscape, SAIC, GTE, RSA, Terisa Systems, and Verisign. SET Secure Electronic Transaction LLC is an organisation that takes care of the management of the SET standard.

Who are the parties involved in SET transactions?
The *cardholder* is the holder of a payment card. In order to participate in SET transactions, he has a 'wallet', i.e., a Cardholder Application at his disposal. The *issuer* is a financial institution that establishes an account for a cardholder and issues a payment card to the cardholder. A *merchant* offers goods or provides services in exchange for payment. An *acquirer* is a finan-

---

[36] However, there is a mechanism in TLS by which TLS 1.0 can emulate SSL 3.0.
[37] SET Secure Electronic Transactions at Visa, <http://www.visa.com/nt/ecomm/set/main.html> (accessed in 2001).

cial institution that establishes an account with a merchant and processes payment card authorisations and payments. A *payment gateway* is a device operated by an acquirer or a designated third party that processes merchant payment messages, including payment instructions from cardholders.

SET enables confidential transfer of messages, it ensures message integrity and authenticates the parties involved in a transaction.[38] SET breaks the whole process of paying for goods or services into several separate transactions, i.e., exchanges of messages between two parties.[39] For these transactions, SET defines protocols. The most prominent transactions are the cardholder registration, the merchant registration, the purchase request, the payment authorisation and the payment capture.[40]

Cardholder and Merchant Registration
In order to send and receive SET messages a cardholder must have a private and public key at his disposal; these are generated by the cardholder's software. Moreover, there must be a CA who holds a certificate linking the cardholder to his public key. The cardholder registration is a transaction between the cardholder and the CA, as a result of which such a certificate comes about, to be held by the CA. The CA, naturally, must be sure that the requester is the person he purports to be; *ergo*, his identity has to be determined. In order to do so, the CA asks the requester 'information such as the cardholder's name, expiration date, account billing address and any additional information the issuing financial institution deems necessary to identify the certificate requester as the valid cardholder'. The CA verifies this information (furnished in the registration request) by comparing it with the cardholder's account information that is kept by the issuer. It is the knowledge of the combination of these data that provides assurance about the

---

[38] SET Secure Electronic Transactions Specification, Book 1: Business Description, p. 3 <http://www.setco.org/download/set_bk1.pdf> (accessed in 2001).

[39] For the description of SET, the Business Description of SET Secure Electronic Transactions Specification has been used as source material.

[40] Apart from the transactions mentioned, SET also provides protocols for other transactions, such as: certificate inquiry and status, purchase inquiry, authorisation reversal, capture reversal, credit, credit reversal, payment gateway certificate request and error messages. See SET Specification, Book 1, p. 31. These transactions are not dealt with in this book.

identity of the requester. Not only a cardholder, but also a merchant must register with a Certificate Authority in order to participate in SET transactions.

The purchase request

This is an exchange of messages between a cardholder and a merchant in which the cardholder sends the order information and the payment instructions to the merchant. The payment instructions are encrypted using the payment gateway's public key. The merchant, who cannot read the payment instructions – forwards them to the payment gateway as part of the payment authorisation.

The payment authorisation

This transaction consists of an exchange of messages between a merchant and an acquirer, in which the merchant seeks authorisation, i.e., a statement by the acquirer that the payment from the cardholder to the merchant may take place.

The payment capture

This transaction also consists of an exchange of messages between a merchant and an acquirer, in which the merchant requests that the payment actually takes place. There may be some lapse of time between the payment authorisation and the actual payment.

For authentication purposes, the transactions do not constitute sessions. This means that every message and every piece of information that needs to have its authenticity verified, is being verified separately. This is done by verifying the digital signature it carries. There is *not* a session, at the beginning of which authenticity is being checked and whereby every message exchanged in the course of the session is deemed to be authentic because of this check at the outset of the session.

Authentication of MIME messages

Multipurpose Internet Mail Extensions (hereinafter: MIME) is a message format for carrying data of any type: text, image, video, sound, etc. A MIME message body may be of the type 'multipart' in which case it contains several bodyparts; each bodypart contains data of a certain type. The MIME

Object Security Services (hereinafter: MOSS) specifies how a digital signature can be appended to data within the MIME format. MOSS does so by defining the structure and processing of messages of the type 'multipart/signed'.[41] A MIME message of this type contains two bodyparts. The first bodypart carries the data that are to be signed, the second part contains the digital signature, an identifier of the algorithm and the parameters, used in the process. To calculate the digital signature, the data are first transformed into canonical form and then signed. The canonical form is an agreed upon notation that ensures that all communicating parties use exactly the same format for the data that are to be signed or have been signed. MOSS is not to be confused with S/MIME, which performs roughly the same function as MOSS, but does so in a technically different way. It uses the PKCS#7 standard for structuring messages.

2.4.4   Technologies covering partial aspects

Timestamps
Digitised data can be copied and modified at will, without leaving traces of the changes that perhaps were made. This of course also holds for a digital indication of date and time. The fact that digital indications of date and time can undetectably be altered lessens the evidentiary value of a digital indication of time in an electronic document. It is possible to upgrade the trust that can be placed in a digital timestamp. This involves the intervention of trusted third parties.

A simple way to create a timestamping service could be to have a trusted party to which one may send a message for timestamping. The trusted party attaches a timestamp to the message and stores the message and stamp in her database. Even better would be to store a hash in the database instead of the entire message. It requires less place and the confidentiality of the message is guaranteed. If at a later point in time there is any need for a corroboration of date and time, it is only a question of verifying the entry in the database of the trusted party.

The PKIX Working Group of the IETF is working on a standard for timestamping.

---

[41] It also defines the type 'multipart/encrypted', which is not dealt with in this book.

Using asymmetric encryption a Time Stamping Authority (hereinafter: TSA) appends a trusted time to a hash of a message and signs the result. It is called a Timestamp token. It establishes the existence of data before a certain point in time. It must however be borne in mind that the existence of the data before a certain time is something else than establishing that data were sent or received. ETSI has formulated standards on a Time Stamping Profile[42] and on Policy Requirements for Time Stamping Authorities.[43]

Cards
Cards have always been used in conjunction with the automated processing of data. At the beginning of computers punch cards were used. Later cards with a magnetic tape came into use. Although magnetic cards were used for a wide variety of purposes, the level of security they offered was low. They were built to a very high degree upon security that was realised by the network they were used in: verifications took place, for example, in an on-line manner. The so-called smartcard took away many of the drawbacks that were inherent in magnetic cards. A smartcard is a credit card sized card with a chip built into it. This chip may merely contain a 'passive' memory, but most modern smartcards have an active memory and a calculation capacity. A number of aspects concerning smartcards have been standardised, such as: the dimensions, the place of the contact surfaces, etc.[44] The functionality of the smartcard, however, depends on the application that has been 'programmed' into it. Many smartcard applications involve authentication, such as: electronic banking, access control, personal identification, etc. The security of smartcards depends on several technical functionalities that the smartcard realises:

- A smartcard can be used to store data. The integrity and confidentiality of the data stored on the card is warranted in that they are only

---

[42] ETSI TS 101 861 v.1.2.1 (2002-03), See <http://pda.etsi.org/exchangefolder/ts_101861v010201p.pdf>, visited in July 2002.
[43] ETSI TS 102 023 v.1.1.1 (2002-04), See <http://pda.etsi.org/exchangefolder/ts_102023v010101p.pdf>, visited in July 2002.
[44] See ISO 7816.

accessible through the smartcard operating system (hereinafter: SCOS). In the SCOS the read and/or write action can be made secure.

- A smartcard allows for off-line verification that the person seeking to use the card is the rightful user of the smartcard. Possession of the card is of course a first indication that the holder is the rightful user of the card. In conjunction with possession, a smartcard mostly offers more advanced means for off-line verification. Fairly common is the use of PIN-codes. A PIN-code, typed in by the user, is matched against data that are securely stored on the card. The verification could also take place by biometric means; the live scan of a bodily characteristic of the person seeking to use the card is then matched against the biometric template that has been stored on the card during enrolment.

- A smartcard is able to authenticate itself towards the terminal it is used in and the terminal can authenticate itself towards the smartcard. This is, *inter alia*, managed by the operating system of the smartcard and makes use of encryption.

- Applications based on the card can offer additional functionalities in the sphere of authentication. As an example one can mention secure on-line communication with the use of the card. A smart card may (depending on the applications it contains) be used in conjunction with symmetric and asymmetric encryption. In this respect 'secure messaging' must be mentioned: the hashing and encryption of messages take place in the card, thus further diminishing the risk that secret keys become compromised.

Chapter 3
USABILITY OF AUTHENTICATION TECHNOLOGY

Chapter 3
USABILITY OF AUTHENTICATION TECHNOLOGY

3.1 INTRODUCTION

Apart from introducing authentication technology to the reader, it is also the aim of this book to explore the usability of authentication technologies. This requires, of course, a perspective from which the usability is to be assessed. As was already stated in the first chapter, the usability is judged from a legal perspective with special emphasis on legal certainty: the usability is greater if the user of authentication technology can better foresee what the legal consequences of the use of authentication technology are. These consequences are especially relevant if the law explicitly binds legal consequences to the use of a signature. In such a case, the user must know under what conditions an electronic signature can be qualified as a signature under the law. This is the first question dealt with in this chapter. The second issue of usability that is addressed in this chapter concerns the evidentiary value of electronic signatures. Both questions will be dealt with under Dutch civil law.

3.2 QUALIFICATION AS A SIGNATURE

3.2.1 Forms of recognition

Before dealing with the question of legal recognition, a preliminary question has to be addressed. Is recognition always relevant? Recognition is certainly relevant if a legal effect is specifically bound to the condition that a signature is used: this is the domain of form requirements. In substantive law, there are several instances in which a signature is a form requirement. According to Article 7:428 DCC on each of the parties to an agency con-

M.H.M. Schellekens, Electronic Signatures
© 2004, ITeR, The Hague, and the author

tract rests, for example, the duty to provide the other party at its request with a *signed* written document that represents the actual contents of the agency contract. According to Article 7:654 DCC, an employer must supply the employee, without charge, with a complete and *signed* copy of the written document with which the employment contract has been concluded or modified. If an electronic signature fails to be recognised as a signature, the signature requirement is not met, and the envisaged legal consequence – such as the materialisation of an agreement – fails to occur. If there is no signature requirement, the presence of a recognised signature may still be relevant, although the consequences of non-recognition may be less black-and-white. The presence or absence of a recognised signature may, for example, be a factor to which to court attaches value when assessing documentary evidence. A signature may also be relevant in the light of form requirements other than a signature requirement. Traditionally, the signature is a means by which an original can be distinguished from a copy. So, theoretically, the presence of a recognised electronic signature could likewise be relevant with respect to the originality requirement. However, we will see later in this chapter that this may be different in the case of electronic signatures. As a last remark, it has to be stated that the recognition of an authentication technology as a signature does not imply that nothing can be wrong with a signature: a traditional handwritten signature can be forged, although it is certainly a signature. Likewise an electronic signature can be placed by an unauthorised person, even though the authentication technology used is recognised as a signature.

In conclusion, the relevance of recognising an electronic signature has in some cases, or may have in other cases, certain legal consequences. Hence, clarity with respect to legal recognition is a prerequisite for legal certainty with respect to electronic signatures.

Now that we have established that recognition is legally relevant, the following question can be addressed: how can a signature be recognised under the law? In the literature, three legislative approaches towards recognition have been discerned. The first approach – the digital signature approach – is the technology-specific approach by which a technology is 'recognised' because it is the technology that is named as the recognised technology. The term 'named' must perhaps not be taken too literally. I consider it to be 'named' not only if the technology is actually named, but also if a description is used that can reasonably only refer to one technology. The second approach – the minimalist approach – gives a less or more general criterion for 'recognition'. The self-evident criterion is that of functional equivalence: if an electronic signature is functionally equivalent to a traditional handwritten signature, it can be used instead of such a handwritten signature. This approach is to a high degree technology neutral, but not completely. The traditional handwritten signature is the prime signature technology; other electronic technologies are only qualifiable as signatures if they are functionally equivalent to the 'prime' signature. So the traditional signature still stands apart as a technology. This is caused by the way in which the recognition of signatures is set up: what holds off-line, is extended to the on-line. Later in this chapter we will see that this set-up has a few consequences. The two-pronged approach is a combination of the two: it combines the legal certainty of the digital signature approach with the technology-neutrality of the second approach by recognising a named technology and accepting other technologies if they meet a certain criterion.

Directive 1999/93/EC chooses the two-pronged approach.[45] The so-called advanced electronic signature based on a qualified certificate is recognised as a 'named' technology. In fact, the digital signature is at present the only technology that can qualify as an advanced electronic signature, based on a qualified certificate. Other technologies can qualify as a signature under the minimalist leg of the two-pronged approach. The relevant 'minimalist' provision reads as follows:

'Member States shall ensure that an electronic signature is not denied legal effectiveness and admissibility as evidence in legal proceedings solely on the grounds that it is:
- in electronic form, or
- not based upon a qualified certificate, or
- not based upon a qualified certificate issued by an accredited certification-service-provider, or
- not created by a secure signature-creation device'.

---

[45] See Directive 1999/93/EC of the European Parliament and of the Council of 13 December 1999 on a Community framework for electronic signatures, Official Journal L 013, 19/01/2000 pp. 0012-0020.

The criterion to be used is however not made explicit in this provision. From the definition of advanced electronic signatures an indication may be derived that the European legislator must have thought about functional equivalence as a criterion. This definition reads as follows: 'electronic signature' means data in electronic form which are attached to or logically associated with other electronic data and which serve as a method of authentication. The definition highlights that an electronic signature is defined as a functional object: it serves 'authentication' purposes, whereby authentication can be understood to be a general indication of the functions of a signature. The Dutch Electronic Signatures Act[46] implementing the directive does name a criterion. The pertinent provision reads as follows in unofficial translation:

> 'An electronic signature has the same legal effect as a handwritten signature, if the method used for authentication is sufficiently reliable, for the purpose for which the electronic data were used, in the light of all the circumstances of the case'.[47]

The provision thus states that qualifiability as a signature ensues if the electronic signature is sufficiently reliable as a method of authentication. Again, authentication can be considered to be a general indication of the function of a signature. So an electronic signature needs to be sufficiently reliable in its functions. That begs the question of what the functions of a signature are. Hereinafter, a number of functions are discerned based on a literature study. The respective functions will be described separately. Knowledge concerning the functions of signatures is helpful in (maybe even a prerequisite for) applying the criterion of sufficient reliability.

---

[46] The complete reference to this Act reads in Dutch: *Wet van 8 mei 2003 tot aanpassing van Boek 3 en Boek 6 van het Burgerlijk Wetboek, de Telecommunicatiewet en de Wet op de economische delicten inzake elektronische handtekeningen ter uitvoering van richtlijn No. 1999/93/EG van het Europees Parlement en de Raad van de Europese Unie van 13 december 1999 betreffende een gemeenschappelijk kader voor elektronische handtekeningen (PbEG L 13) (Wet elektronische handtekeningen), Staatsblad 2003, 199.*

[47] The original text (inserted in the Dutch Civil Code as Art. 6:227a) reads in Dutch as follows: *Een elektronische handtekening heeft dezelfde rechtsgevolgen als een handgeschreven handtekening, indien de methode die daarbij is gebruikt voor authentificatie voldoende betrouwbaar is, gelet op het doel waarvoor de elektronische gegevens werden gebruikt en op alle overige omstandigheden van het geval.'

3.2.2 The functions of a signature

Hereinafter, six functions of signatures are discerned: authentication, identification, authorisation, integrity, originality and the cautionary function. The description of each function is structured in the following way: with respect to each function, first it is explained what the function means. Once the meaning of a function is established, the relevance of the function in substantive law and its relevance in an evidentiary setting are described.

Authentication
What is it?
Authentication is the act of the authenticator by which he earmarks a document as being authentic and in doing so confirms its authenticity. The authenticity concerns several aspects of the signed document:

- Authenticity with respect to the person of the authenticator. This is closely related to the identificatory function and will be dealt with in the next section.
- Authenticity with respect to the declaration. The signature signifies that the declaration that is above it, is the declaration as the signatory has made or accepted it; acceptance refers to the situation in which the signatory accepts a statement that stems from somebody else.
- Authenticity with respect to the contents of the declaration. This means that, according to the signatory, the contents of the declaration correspond to his will, to the result of prior oral negotiations or in general to what the signatory is willing to express or to accept. The signature of a secretary under the minutes of a meeting signifies, for example, that according to the secretary, the minutes are a good representation of what has been said or decided during the meeting. This example highlights another point in that the authenticity of the contents of the declaration does not concern 'the objective truth' (if such a thing exists at all), but rather 'a truth' to which the signatory is willing to commit him or herself.

In the literature, the latter aspect of authenticity is often referred to as the adoption of the contents of a declaration as one's own and as the appropriation of the declaration.[48,49] Appropriation and adoption both involve a mental aspect, the animus signandi. The affixing of the signature is the externally perceptible act by which the animus signandi is expressed. The (supposed) presence of an animus signandi means that the signature is not a simple physical act, but is considered as something by which the authenticity of the document is expressed and confirmed. What the legal consequence of such an expression is, or can be, is something that is discussed in the next section concerning substantive law and evidence.

The term 'authentication' has a second meaning that differs from what has been said above: authentication is the successful verification of identity or authority.[50] This meaning of authentication is prevalent in computer science literature. In computer science, authentication is the means of gaining confidence that remote people or things are who or what they claim to be.[51] For example, data are authenticated if their origin has been successfully verified.

Meaning in substantive law
The signature is a token of the 'adoption' of the contents of the declaration; it is up to substantive law to determine what the legal significance of the adoption is.

Placing one's signature under a document may in many ways be relevant in substantive law. I will confine myself to what is probably the most general function in civil law. Placing a signature may qualify as making a declaration of one's will. The term declaration has a special position within Dutch civil law, since a declaration of one's will (directed at bringing about a certain legal consequence) is the means to perform a

---

[48] From an analysis of English caselaw, Reed distills three functions for a signature; it provides evidence of the identity of the signatory, that the signatory intended the signature to be his signature and that the signatory approves of and adopts the contents of the document. See Reed 2000, section 3.1.3.

[49] Dumortier and Van den Eynde discern the double function of the identification of the signatory and the appropriation of the contents of the signed document by the signatory. See Dumortier and Van den Eynde 2001, p. 187.

[50] See, e.g., Angel 1999, section 2.1. Here, 'authentication' is defined as: to authenticate the identity of the person who signed the data so it is known who participated in the transaction.

[51] See Ford and Baum 1997, p. 126.

legal act. In general, such a declaration can be made in any form. There-fore, there is, in my view, no reason why signing a document could not be considered to be a method of declaration. By signing and thus authen-ticating a document a person can formally declare. The declaration can be thought to be concentrated in the act of signing or authenticating. On the other hand, it has to be pointed out that there are other ways (e.g., orally or tacitly) to make a declaration. Authenticating a document is not an ex-clusive means of declaration. If there are oral negotiations preceding the signing there may even arise discussion as to whether the oral or the signed statements constitute 'the' declaration. This is especially relevant if somebody contends that the written statements in the document diverge from what was orally discussed.

In the literature sometimes the completion or finalisation function of signatures is mentioned when discussing this aspect of signing. In soci-ety, it is understood that a declaration in a document has no legal mean-ing as long as it has not been signed. Placing the signature(s) makes it complete or final. This means, e.g., that through signing, the 'legal act' has come about and that a means to prove the fact is created. If the legal act came about through oral negotiations, the coming into existence of the legal act is of course not an effect of the finalisation or completion.

Bringing about a legal act is not the only way in which signing is rel-evant in substantive law. As an example, one can think of the secretary mentioned above. A secretary who signs a record of a meeting thus im-plicitly declares that, in her opinion, the record correctly represents what has been said and decided upon at the meeting. This implicit declaration results in the fact that a wilful misrepresentation of the facts is unlawful and may give rise to liability.

Evidence

Although the signature does confirm the authenticity of a document, the question whether a court that has to decide on the authenticity of the docu-ment is willing or even obliged to accept the authenticity on account of the presence of the signature is another matter.

In answering this question according to Dutch law, one first needs to decide whether the signed document can be considered to be a private in-strument, an authentic deed or neither of the aforementioned. With re-spect to the evidentiary value of the private instrument and the authentic deed the Dutch Code of Civil Procedure lays down a few rules. An instrument or deed is a signed written document, meant to serve as evidence.[52] An authentic deed is an instrument that has been drawn up in the prescribed form by a competent civil servant who, by an Act or implementing decree, is commissioned in this way to provide evidence his observations or acts. A private instrument is then simply defined as an instrument that is not an authentic deed. For an instrument to have its special evidentiary value (see below), it must be in the original form.[53]

A private instrument does not have special evidentiary standing with respect to the identity of the signatory. The person whose signature appears to be beneath the document is held to be the signatory as long as his signature is not positively denied (by himself or a legal successor). Once denied, the private instrument does not have evidentiary value as long as it remains unproven who placed the signature beneath the document. With respect to an authentic instrument on the other hand, a court must hold the party whose signature appears to be on the document to be the signatory, unless proof to the contrary is adduced.

An authentic deed provides proof of the integrity of the text above the signature. Whoever contends that the text above the signature has been altered after signing, must adduce proof of his contention. A private instrument does not provide evidence of the integrity of the text above the signature. If the integrity is disputed the private instrument is in limbo.

Both a private and an authentic instrument provide proof of the authenticity of the truth of the statement above the signature, for the opposing party of the party against whom the instrument is meant to provide proof. An authentic deed also provides compulsory proof for everyone of whatever the public servant has declared within the ambit of his authority concerning his own actions and observations. A court must accept the proof provided by the instrument, unless proof to the contrary is adduced.

If a signed document is neither of the aforementioned, a court is in principle free to assess the evidentiary value it is willing to attribute to the document with respect to the three aspects of authenticity discerned

---

[52] See Art. 183 Dutch Code of Civil Procedure (hereinafter: DCCP).

[53] In some special circumstances, copies of an authentic deed have the same evidentiary value as originals. See Art. 187 DCCP.

above. However, society has laid the foundation for the evidentiary value of signatures. In society, signing has been given the meaning of committing oneself to what is signed, the signatory knows that important legal consequences can ensue when signing. A court – when called upon to decide on the evidentiary value of a document – may not ignore these circumstances.

Identification

In order to understand the identificatory function of signatures, it first needs to be understood what an identity is. On this basis, an identity is that which ensures that one is who one claims to be. It is the entirety of one's personal characteristics, one's personality. The term 'identity' refers to 'the properties that characterise an entity', its personality, individuality or singularity. The fact that everybody has an identity of his own means that everybody is unique and therefore in principle distinguishable as an individual entity, different from all other entities. Although rarely made explicit, the existence of unique identities is something which the law strongly builds upon. Many legal constructions could not function if people were not identifiable. The law holds, for example, persons responsible for their acts on an individual basis. Individual responsibility presupposes that persons can be distinguished from each other. Apart from the aspect of distinguishability, an identity conveys information about a person. Personal characteristics are, because of their particularity, information rich.[54] Especially if this information can be determinative for the way in which somebody is treated, it is legally relevant; think, for example, of informational privacy that seeks to regulate the use of such information in the interest of the person concerned.

In day to day life, a complete view of somebody's identity (all of a person's exclusive traits) is non-existent. How could you tell that your perception is all encompassing? In practice, you have at most a limited view of somebody else's individuality. This is even more so in an on-line environment in which a person can participate without showing much of him or herself. So, in practice, other people have to make do with a rather

---

[54] The more unexpected a message is, the more information it confers. Particular characteristics are, because of their peculiarity, their being out of the ordinary prime candidates for unexpected message contents.

limited view of somebody's identity: the identity as it is perceived by third persons, which can be considered to be a second meaning of identity. The limited nature of a third person's views, the bias that is possibly introduced by the subjectivity of their perception, may or may not impinge the functions which an identity has. The limited nature of such a view and the subjectivity may or may not compromise the identifiability, depending on whether the particular view allows sight of enough traits that are sufficiently intersubjective to unambiguously distinguish the person in question. The completeness and possible bias probably do have a bearing on the 'information' function of an identity. These limitations and the openness of the identity concept mean that an identity is not as such, and without further steps, suitable for many operational purposes. For many practical, legal and especially signing purposes, a need exists to be able to easily refer to, address, individualise and recognise persons. A (description of one's) perceived personality is too cumbersome and probably too ambiguous for these purposes. An identity in any of the above senses (the idealistic total view, or the more realistic limited perception) has therefore little operational value when considering the identificatory function of signatures. The needs of day to day life require a short and easy to use 'handle' to an individual person. This handle is in the first place found in one's name. The name stresses the individualisation aspect of an identity; the information aspect is very less prevalent in a name, but may not be completely absent; a name may, for example, give information concerning the foreign descent of its bearer. One's name, possibly accompanied by other data such as one's Christian names, the date and place of birth, height and eye colour, is also called someone's identity, perhaps because the name takes the place of a description of one's identity. A signature is in principle a handwritten name and in this way it gives direct access to one's identity.

Slowly but surely, human readable data other than one's name have appeared and started to function as identities. User names, social security numbers, employee numbers, perhaps e-mail addresses, etc., may be considered as identities in the same sense as a name can be considered to be an identity. Whether some of these identities also amount to being signatures, is dealt with in the next chapter.

An identity, in its meaning as a short handle to a person, exhibits a third aspect, apart from its identificatory and informational function. This third element is its status. Not all identifying information is an identity. A handle needs to acquire a status as an identity. What is needed for a handle to obtain the status of identity is dependent upon the context in which it is to be used. Sometimes, the law indicates what can function as an identity. In the case of statutory identification duties, the law indicates with which documents one can identify oneself. The personal data mentioned in these documents indicate what constitutes an identity. In the case of signatures, less far-reaching demands are placed on identities. A signature may, for example, also indicate a pseudonym: Directive 1999/93/EC forbids Member States to prevent certification service providers from indicating in the certificate a pseudonym instead of the signatory's name.[55] Whether a signatory can actually sign with a pseudonym does of course again depend on the purpose for which the signature is to be used.

Identification is the determination or verification of which identity belongs to somebody. For verification purposes a means of identification is often used. A means of identification is something that allows a 'claimed' association of an identity with a person to be verified.

A means of identification ideally has the following properties.
- It has to be unique, i.e., it has to differ from other people's means of identification. Different persons have different signatures.
- It points to the person that is to be identified. For example, a signature represents the name of the signatory or it is otherwise known to belong to somebody.
- The person identified by the means of identification is the only person that can create the means of identification, or his or her co-operation is necessary.

A fingerprint may be a means of identification:
- Everybody has a different fingerprint.
- If one has a database at one's disposal that links fingerprints to people's identities, one can say that a fingerprint points to its owner.
- Only the 'owner' of a fingerprint can put his fingerprint on an object.

---

[55] See Art. 8.3 Directive 1999/93/EC under the provision that non-prevention does not prejudice the legal effect given to pseudonyms under national law.

Also a signature is a means of identification, hence its capability to identify the signatory is explained. It is however a question whether a signature necessarily needs to possess each of the three mentioned properties. Especially the latter seems to be restrictive; considering the third property to be mandatory may exclude all authentication technologies that do not use biometric technologies.

Substantive meaning
Since a signature has an identificatory function, it may provide or confirm knowledge of the signatory's identity. There are many circumstances in which it is of importance to a contracting party – or an aspirant contracting party – to know the identity of the other (aspirant) party. The knowledge of the identity may, for example, serve certain purposes, such as exercising one's freedom to choose who is to become one's contracting party; this is especially pertinent if the person of the contracting party is a deciding factor. In *Hofland* v. *Hennis*, the recognition of the interest that a seller of a house has in knowing the (aspirant) buyer's identity was a deciding factor in the court's decision to hold that an advert for selling a house did not legally qualify as an offer, but merely as an invitation to negotiate. Furthermore, knowledge of identity can be relevant in substantive law in deciding whether a contract can be rescinded on the basis of 'error in persona'.[56] Fraud may be based on incorrect information about one's identity provided to the victim. A signature is, because of its identificatory function in these cases, merely the means by which knowledge of an identity is conveyed. Strictly speaking, it is not the signature, but knowledge of an identity or the provision of a false identity that is determinative for the resulting legal consequences. On the Internet, signatures become perhaps a more important source of identity knowledge than in a traditional environment, since other clues to a party's identity (the shop window) are less prevalent or trustworthy.

The identificatory function of a signature is closely connected to its authentication function: it is necessary to know who authenticated a

---

[56] For the former see, e.g., HR (Dutch Supreme Court) 10 April 1980, NJ 1981, 532 (*Hennis* v. *Hofland*), for the latter see, e.g., Kantongerecht (Subdistrict Court) 7 April 1977, NJ 1977, 582 (*Bakker* v. *Terpstra*).

document. Apart from authentication settings a signature may also be used for independent identificatory purposes.

Evidentiary significance

A signature is the prime means to prove the identity of the signatory. This does not mean, however, that a court is in all circumstances obliged to assign to a signature a high evidentiary value with respect to the identity of the signatory. As we have seen above under the heading 'authentication', the probative value with respect to the identity of the signatory depends on whether the writing is an authentic deed, a private instrument or neither of the two. In the two latter cases, a (positive) denial of the signature is enough to rob the signature of its probative value with respect to the identity of the signatory. Proof of who placed the signature beneath the document reinstates the probative value. An authentic deed on the other hand, does have probative value with respect to the identity of the signatory. In order to undermine its probative value, proof to the contrary has to be adduced; a positive denial is not enough.

With respect to terminology, the following must be mentioned. A purported signatory can deny his signature. Such a denial is called repudiation. Depending on the role of the signatory – does he himself declare or does he accept somebody else's declaration – repudiation is divided into repudiation of origin and repudiation of receipt. The repudiation can be a truthful denial (the signature is a forgery) or it can be untruthful (the signatory regrets having signed).

Authorisation

What is it?

Under the law, the term 'authorisation' has more than one meaning. A first meaning is the following. By signing a document containing a declaration, the signatory declares implicitly that he is authorised to make the declaration and to perform the associated legal act. This aspect of authorisation especially comes to light if the signatory actually lacks authority to act. The fact that the signature has been placed under the false pretence of being authorised to do so, offers a basis for holding the 'signatory' liable for (possible) damages. The false pretence of being authorised is deduced from the very use of the signature by the unauthorised party.

Secondly, the term 'authorisation' may also be used to indicate a successful verification of somebody's authority to do something. Verification is the checking of a claim, e.g., a claim of identity or authority. Verification can take place in one of various settings, e.g., before a transaction takes place, or in an evidentiary setting. By showing that a person is able to produce his signature, he can convince a verifier that he is the 'owner' of the signature. To make the verification complete, the verifier must have reference data at his disposal that associate a signature with such authority (to do something) or possibly an identity. When paying with a cheque one often has to demonstrate one's authority to perform payments with the cheque and a corresponding banker's card. By signing the cheque and allowing the recipient of the payment to compare the signature on the cheque with that on the banker's card, the payer enables the recipient to verify his authority to use the payment instrument. An example from Dutch caselaw is the following: a bank paid cash to a person who showed his 'postidentiteitsbewijs', i.e., an ID card. The bank did not verify the signature. Verification of the signature would have brought to light that he was not authorized to draw money from the account in question.[57] The bank was found to be liable. In computer science, the term 'authorisation' is mainly used to indicate a (successful) verification of authority. A verification of authority may, for example, take place in the context of guarding access to a resource (such as a network, data, computer capacity, etc.).

Finally, authorisation may be used within the meaning of giving authority, e.g., I may authorise somebody to act on my behalf, in my name; authorisation then has the meaning of 'granting power of attorney'. If the authorisation is in writing and signed, the signature is no more than a means to finalise a declaration and, thereby, to perform the legal act of granting a power of attorney. Finalising a declaration as a purpose for using signatures has been dealt with under the heading 'authentication'. Authorisation in this sense is merely an instance of the more general function of authentication, as described above.

Substantive meaning: The implicit declaration of authority is an argument or basis for laying the consequences of unauthorised signing at the doorstep

---

[57] Hof (Court of Appeal) Amsterdam 12 November 1992, NJ 1994, 513 (Bolwerk/ CVB).

of the unauthorised signer. In this respect a parallel can be drawn with Article 3:70 DCC. According to this provision, a person acting with a power of attorney, must vouch to the other party for the existence and scope of the power, unless the opposing party knows or ought to understand that an adequate power is lacking or unless the person has notified the opposing party of the entire substance of the granted power.

Evidentiary meaning: The (existence of the) signature can be understood to be evidence of the implicit declaration of authority. Furthermore, the act of signing in front of the eyes of a verifier is a way of convincing the verifier of one's 'ownership' of a signature.

Integrity or authenticity
What is it?
Integrity indicates that data in a document have not been altered, deleted or supplemented, irrespective of whether this has come about through natural causes or through manipulation. Integrity compares data at two points in time: are the data still the same as when they where first stored? Against a breach of integrity a handwritten signature offers some protection. As the signature is directly under the text, it is difficult to add something inconspicuously. Apart from this meaning, integrity may also be used in a second meaning, i.e., in the sense of authenticity. Integrity in this second sense means that a document correctly represents the statements of the signatory. In this sense, integrity sees to the correspondence between the will, the oral statements, the knowledge of the signatory, on the one hand, and the (correct) representation thereof in the document on the other. The signature constitutes confirmation of this correspondence. One could also say that a signatory authenticates a document, because he has convinced himself of its authenticity.

Substantive meaning: For integrity in its former sense, it is difficult to discern a specific function in substantive law. The signature is a safeguard against an attack on integrity. This might be a reason for the legislator to require a signature as a form requirement. If it does so, the integrity does play in an indirect way a role in substantive law: legal consequence may ensue if the form requirement of a signature has not been met.

Evidentiary meaning: With respect to integrity in its former sense, it was remarked above that the signature offers some protection against a breach of integrity. As such a signature may have a positive influence on the assessment of the evidentiary value of a signed document by the judge or arbitrator. With respect to integrity in the sense of authenticity, the evidentiary function is closely related to the authentication function. By signing, a signatory implicitly declares that he has convinced himself of the fact that the statements in the signed document conform to his will, etc. This may act as an argument in favour of the position that his signature is a token of his informed consent.

Originality
What is it?
Originality refers to the characteristic that a document is an original, i.e., that it is not a copy. Speaking of 'originality' therefore presupposes that originals and copies are distinguishable. It is often the presence of a hand-written signature that marks a document as an original. Also, the imperfections in traditional copying technologies, such as photocopiers and faxes, enable one to distinguish between originals and copies.
Substantive meaning: Originality is a vital property if a document acts as the embodiment of possessory rights in goods, such as is the case with a bill of lading. An original bill of lading identifies its possessor as the person entitled to the delivery of the cargo. A document of title must be relatively unique and originality is a means to ensure this.
Evidentiary meaning: Originality heightens the evidentiary value of a document. The special evidentiary value that is attached to private instruments and authentic deeds is confined to instruments and deeds that are in their 'original' form (Article 160.1 DCCP). The distinguishability of originals and copies makes forgery more difficult.

Cautionary function and taking notice of the contents of the document
Placing one's signature is generally understood to be an act that does entail relevant legal consequences. A person may therefore think twice before he places his signature under a document. He is thereby encouraged to take notice of the document he is about to sign. The signature can thus be said to have the function of a caution that safeguards signatories from an overly rash entry into legal acts. Some point out that the cautionary function is not a general function of signatures, because the normative aspect is lacking. There is no general duty to use a signature, and thus the safeguard against

rash decisions comes to hang in the balance.[58] I would however like to approach the question of the cautionary function from the other side. If a signature has been used it can be said to have exerted its cautionary influence, thus affirming the cautionary function of signatures. The advantage of this approach is apparent, if one considers the evidentiary value of this function.

Meaning in substantive law: by placing one's signature, the signatory implicitly declares that he has taken notice of the contents of the document he signs. In some cases, a 'normal' consent is not enough, but a qualified consent is required. Under English law, Reed attributes to signatures the function of being evidence of a consumer's *informed* consent to the transaction he has entered to.[59] Furthermore, the cautionary aspect may be a reason for the legislator to require the signed form for certain legal acts.

Evidentiary value: Because of the cautionary effect of signing, it can very well be deduced that the signatory was aware of what he was signing and must have had the intention to enter into the legal act as he did. Thus, the cautionary function contributes to the evidentiary value of signatures.

3.2.3 Performing the functions with the help of technology

Given the functions of a signature as described above, it will now be determined whether the technologies described in chapter 2 are suited to performing the functions. The treatment of the capability of technologies to perform the functions will be structured along the lines of the technologies. This is the way in which the issues present themselves in practice. The legal functions often show a great deal of coherence, and may therefore lend themselves less to an isolated treatment. The way in which different functions are performed by one technology will not prove to be disjunctive. Functions are seamlessly interwoven. The technologies will hereinafter be dealt with in the order in which they appeared in chapter 2.

---

[58] See Reed 2000, section 3.2.2 entitled: 'Consumer protection?'
[59] See Reed 2000, section 3.2.2.

3.2.3.1 *Technologies for network identification*

The prime functionality of MAC addresses, IP addresses, domain names and URIs are the identification of equipment or data in a computer network. They are often registered in the name of a person, but activities undertaken under such banner are in themselves not enough to conclude that the registered person endorses the actions of, or the information that is made available from the computer carrying the MAC address, IP address or domain name. In many cases it is not even the registered person who makes information available or 'acts' through the computer.

The e-mail address that indicates the sender of an e-mail message may by its composition suggest the identity of a specific person. If it does, the use of the address may in the first place have a functional background: enabling the recipient to see from whom the message stems and enabling him or her to reply. A question is whether the indication of the sender's e-mail address can – under certain circumstances – be read to mean authentication of the contents of the e-mail messages. Authentication presupposes an intentional act directed at the confirmation of the authenticity of the message. In society, the sending of an e-mail message is not associated with such explicit authentication of the message. This does not however detract from the fact that under the law, a statement can be imputed to a person on the basis of an e-mail message sent by him and the same e-mail message may provide or contribute to the proof of the statement. An explicit act of authentication is generally not required. If, for the sake of some form requirement, it is necessary to decide whether a meaningful act of authentication has taken place, the circumstances of the case have to be considered. Such circumstances may be derived from factors such as the content of the message, the nature of the relationship between the sender and the recipient, and previous agreements between the parties.

Since network identification technologies merely identify resources, there is no guarantee with respect to the integrity of the data. Sometimes, only the address of the resource is indicated, with no guarantees concerning what may be found at the address. But even if a technology (such as a DOI) directly refers to the resource, its integrity may only be guaranteed by additional technical or organisational measures.

As a conclusion, one can say that the use of these technologies may be helpful in imputing actions or statements to a person, but may in themselves not be enough to conclude such an imputation. Having said this, it goes without saying that these technologies have in general no special standing with respect to authentication in society; the use of such technology is not considered as something to which important legal consequences are bound.

3.2.3.2 *Passwords and PINs*

The identificatory capabilities of passwords and PINs seem at first sight to be limited. A password may, for example, not conform to the requirement of uniqueness: many persons may be using the same password. In the case of a PIN, the uniqueness is often relative. We all have a four-digit PIN that goes with our banker's card; this four-digit string allows at most 10,000 different (i.e., unique) PINs. As the number of bank customers is a multiplicity of 10,000, some people are bound to have the same PIN as other people. Uniqueness cannot therefore be attained with the four digits of the PIN alone. Furthermore, passwords and PINs are handed out to a unique person, who has to keep his or her password or PIN secret. The organisation handing out the password or PIN often – for security reasons – does not register the PIN.[60] This aspect also seems to hamper the identificatory function of PINs and passwords, since this practice seems to make it difficult, if not impossible, to relate them to usable identities. The function of the PIN in this case is rather to allow verification of the user's authority to use the card. With respect to the identification function, it is no more than a building block. The actual identification and uniqueness are attained with the help of additional data, such as a bank account number or a user name. The PIN or the password must merely ensure that the person typing in the password or PIN is actually the same as the person identified with the help of additional data. The case of the PIN serves well to illustrate that the functions – in this case identification and authorisation – can be interwoven.

The question of authentication is (again) to a high degree dependent upon the context in which the technology is used. If a combination of a

---

[60] Verification takes place off-line, e.g., with the help of data contained on a card.

username and a password merely serves to guard access to a closed network, its function is rather authorisation than authentication. Offering a
banker's card to an ATM and typing in one's PIN code, does, in my
view, have an authentication function. The actions authenticate the payment order that is thereafter given to the bank. The fact that the typing in
of the password or PIN takes place at a time when the actions time to be
authenticated still have to be formulated, is in my view not an impedi-
ment for that position. What the user is going to authenticate is foresee-
able and can be determined by the user.

Integrity (and if applicable originality) are functions that are
performed by security which is built into the technical environment (network, smartcard, etc.) in which the password or PIN is used. This shows
that passwords and PINs cannot always be used in isolation, but a need
may exist to interweave them with the technical and organisational context in which they are used. The cautionary function may, on the one
hand, build on the fact that the typing in of a password or PIN requires a
conscious act by the person in question. However, the user interface that
sets the 'scene' in which the password or PIN is typed has an important
role as well. On the one hand, it may undo any cautionary effect. If the
user interface offers the option of 'remembering' the password for conve-
nience sake, the cautionary effect is lost. On the other hand, the user
interface may be programmed to enhance the cautionary element. It may
require that passwords be retyped, it may indicate clearly what the meaning and implications are of entering a password or PIN, it may be clearly
structured so as to contribute to understandability, it may clearly indicate
the moment at which irreversible steps are taken etc. Here again, it is
clear that technical elements cannot be viewed in their isolation, if it
comes to a legal assessment.

3.2.3.3   *Biometric technology*

Identification
Biometric technology is in principle suitable for identifying the signatory.
The corporal feature is chosen in such a way that its uniqueness is sufficiently guaranteed. A live scan as such does not amount to an identity. There
must be a capability to translate the live scan to a real world identity.

Authentication
The capacity of biometric technologies for authentication purposes depends upon the context in which biometrics are used. Some applications of biometrics, such as guarding access to a building, may have nothing to do with authentication.[61] Other applications of biometric technologies may play a role in composite authentication technology; biometrics may, for example, guard access to a private key. Still other technologies, such as dynamic signatures, are designed as substitutes for signatures, and will in society be perceived as authentication devices. In the latter case, the biometric template generated during the act of signing is however not attached to the data that have been authenticated. A biometric template is from a privacy perspective too sensitive and an authentication technology based on biometric verification may become too vulnerable, if biometric templates would find a wide dispersal through their presence in signed documents. This means that dynamic signatures depend to a high degree on security built into the technical environment (e.g., the network) in which they are used.

Biometrics still seem to be suffering from limited reliability. However, by combining biometric technology with other technologies, such as PINs, adequate reliability may be attained.

Authorisation
Biometric technology can be used for authorisation purposes, e.g., access to a smartcard may be guarded with biometric technologies. An authorisation need not necessarily be accompanied by identification.

'If biometrics are for instance used for guarding access to a building, the only thing that needs to be established when somebody seeks access to the building is whether he may enter the building or not. The live scan only needs to match a template in a list of templates belonging to persons who are authorised to access the building. Who the persons are to whom these templates belong, need not be established when a person seeks access to the building. It only needs to be established whether his template matches a template in the list. The only output of the verification is "yes or no". It must

---

[61] This does not detract from the fact that an authentication can be construed: by offering one's corporal feature to be checked one authenticates the implicit request to gain entry to the building.

nevertheless be borne in mind that in the back-office the data to translate biometric templates to a "usable" identity will most probably be retained.[62] It
must after all be possible to strike somebody off the list of persons who may
have access to the building'.

Integrity and originality
Biometric technology cannot deliver support for guaranteeing the integrity
or originality of statements and documents. For these purposes, biometric
technologies have to be combined with other technologies.

Cautionary function
Dynamic signature technologies often incorporate the feature that the image of the signature can be placed on a document. For the perception of the
user, a paper situation is thus emulated quite accurately. This may arguably
contribute to its capability to exert a cautionary effect.

3.2.3.4   Symmetric encryption

Identification
An encryption key as such has no meaning. An identificatory capacity of
symmetric encryption depends on assumptions concerning who has a key
at his exclusive disposal and on an assumption concerning the checks that
have been made before the distribution of the keys.[63] If a key is used by no
more than two parties who keep the key secret, symmetric encryption is in
principle suitable for identification between the two parties. Such application of symmetric encryption does not support non-repudiation, however. If
one party denies having sent or received a document, the production of the
opposing party of the document encrypted with the symmetric key does not

---

[62] In the enrollment phase, the link between identity and template is established and
probably stored.

[63] In the case of symmetric encryption, the communicating parties both need to have
the secret key at their disposal. Key distribution is therefore a necessity, but it is not supported by symmetric encryption. Symmetric encryption is often used in conjunction with
public key encryption. The symmetric key is then exchanged in a handshake session that
is secured with the help of asymmetric encryption (think, for example, of SSL). In the
handshake session, a master key is exchanged. With the help of the master key, the session keys can be generated.

prove sending or receiving by the other party: the opposing party could have attached the symmetric key himself.

Authentication

Symmetric encryption may be used in an authentication function. Whether this is the case must be deduced from the nature of the application of symmetric encryption. Keyed hash functions can be used to establish a link between the document and the authenticator.

Authorisation

Symmetric encryption can be used for the verification of authorisation. A person seeking an authorisation may be asked to demonstrate possession of the symmetric key, e.g., by showing that he can decrypt a random message.

Integrity and originality

Symmetric encryption can be used for the verification of integrity. If a message has itself been encrypted, decryption will reveal any alteration between sending and receiving; the clear text will be nonsensical. If a MAC has been used the sent MAC and the MAC newly calculated over the message as received will not add up. For the determination of originality, symmetric encryption does not offer support.

Cautionary function

As with many other authentication technologies, the cautionary aspect can better be dealt with by other technologies, such as sophisticated user interfaces.

3.2.3.5   Digital signatures

Identification

A digital signature as such has no meaning. It obtains its meaning from the fact that certain information – an identity or an authorisation – is linked to the public key in a certificate. The meaning of the information in the certificate is therefore of primordial importance for the identificatory function. Upon enrolment sufficient measures must be taken to ensure that the information, e.g., the identity to public key binding, is correct, that the key-pair is only used by one person and that the person requesting the certificate has the complementary private key at his disposal. The user of the private key – the 'owner' of the digital signature – must keep his private key confidential, so that he is in a unique position to create his digital signature. Given the great importance that this exclusive control of the private key represents, technology often offers users support for maintaining its confidentiality. PIN codes, biometric technologies and smartcards are called upon to ensure that only the rightful holder of a private key is able to use it. A smartcard might not only protect access to a private key, it may also perform the encryption; in that case the private key does not have to leave the smartcard itself.

Authentication
Technically, asymmetric encryption and its main application, digital signatures, are suitable for performing the authentication function. With the help of a hash a digital signature can be logically bound to a document. Whether a particular use of asymmetric encryption amounts to authentication depends on the meaning that can be given to the use of the technology in the circumstances of the case. A Certification Practise Statement provides an insight into what the data in the certificate mean and thus sheds some light on the 'meaning' of the digital signature. The 'name' of the technology may provide further indications of the intended use of the technology. Calling a technology 'digital signature' facilitates that its use is perceived as 'signing'. Calling a certificate a 'server certificate' indicates that it merely shows what the 'identity' of a server is. Such a certificate may also indicate who the manager of the server is, but it does not necessarily identify the sender of messages that originate from the server or web sites that are made available from the server.

Authorisation
As we saw, with the identificatory function, the information in the certificate shows whether an application of asymmetric encryption is used for authorisation purposes. A certificate may alternately or additionally to an identification contain an authorisation. An authorisation need not be enjoined by an identification. In a suitable setting one may 'prove' one's authorisation by demonstrating one's possession of the private key, without revealing it.

Integrity
Asymmetric encryption is very suitable for the guarantee of integrity. A digital signature is calculated over a hash of the signed document. This does not prevent manipulation of the document, but ensures that any manipulation will be discovered when verifying the signature. Also the opposite holds true: if the document is not manipulated this fact is confirmed by the signature. Furthermore, the hash ensures that a signature cannot be 'attached' to another document.

Originality
If originality with respect to digital data is defined as the set of data that is the first to come into being, it is not possible to distinguish originals from copies with the help of asymmetric encryption or a digital signature. Additional technologies are needed. A timestamp may be helpful in the determination of originality.

Cautionary function
The technology of asymmetric encryption does not particularly support the cautionary aspect. Factors that may be relevant are: is human intervention required for the affixing of a digital signature (or is there perhaps a software agent that performs this autonomously?) and the way in which the user interface is laid out.

3.2.3.6   *SSL and TLS*

SSL and TLS certify a server and optionally a client. The server (more precisely its IP address or domain name) may be registered in the name of some natural or legal person. Such registration generally does not mean that actions of the server are imputable to this person. This is especially so if the server is being used for hosting content of a third party.

SSL is concerned with the authentication of servers and securing communication channels. Messages that are sent using an SSL connection are encrypted using symmetric encryption techniques. This considerably complicates manipulations of the contents of messages.

3.2.3.7 *Timestamps and Cards*

A timestamp only registers when a certain act has taken place. As such it is too limited in scope to function as a signature. As an additional technology, it has a supportive role with respect to integrity and originality. With the help of a timestamp it may be possible to determine whether a message has been sent twice or has merely arrived twice due to a technical error during transportation. A timestamp may be useful in establishing non-repudiation of origin.

Cards as such are not signatures of course, but they support other technologies.

With respect to identification and authorisation, they are helpful in that they may help to verify that the person seeking to use the card is actually authorised to do so. A card may, for example, contain a biometrical template or a PIN. Also data printed on the card (readable with the naked eye) such as a photograph of the cardholder reinforce this function.

Cards may be helpful with respect to authentication aspects in that they may contain data that enable authentication, e.g., a private key or a 'symmetric' key. As has been described in the technical chapter, a smartcard operating system supports strong access control. It is through the prohibition of unauthorised access that the integrity of the data stored on the card is retained.

Possibly, originality may be supported by the use of certain smartcards in that they allow data on a card to be used only once. Card applications featuring this capacity are not widely used – if they exist at all.

3.2.4 **The functions of and qualification as a signature**

The fact that a signature has more than one function, raises the question whether an electronic signature can only be qualified as a signature if it fulfils all signature functions. This is not the case. From the requirements that the Directive and the Dutch Electronic Signatures Act use for advanced electronic signatures it is apparent that authentication and identification are the prime functions of a signature. Whether other functions need to be met comes to depend on the individual case in which a signature is to be applied. If a signature is used in order to conform to a form requirement, the form requirement itself and its rationale can give further indications of what functions need to be fulfilled and with what degree of reliability.

Apart from determining which functions must be fulfilled, there is the question of the reliability with which a function is to be performed by the electronic signature.

This determination is complicated and hinges on the specifics of the case at hand. It involves the following:

- The form requirement itself: What is its rationale?
- The case at hand: What is at stake? What is the value of the transaction or the dispute?
- The authentication technology: How resistant is the technology against natural or man-made attacks against its integrity and availability? The latter may usually require an assessment by a technician. The court may thus have to be advised.
- Parties may agree upon a level of reliability. Such agreement can, however, not undo the criterion given in the Dutch Electronic Signatures Act: parties cannot agree upon a level of reliability that does not meet the threshold, laid down in the Act.[64]

3.2.5   What is beyond functional equivalence?

According to the Dutch Electronic Signatures Act, an electronic signature can be qualified as the functional equivalent of a traditional signature if it is sufficiently reliable as a method for authentication. This is an open texture that needs to be filled in a concrete case. The form requirement and its rationale give direction to this 'filling in'. Functional equivalence may thus have different implications with respect to different form requirements and in different situations. This may mean that a varying set of functions of signatures is involved in the determination of functional equivalence. All this, however, presupposes that a functionally equivalent electronic signature is the best way to deal with the form requirement. Even more so, it is assumed that it is always possible to find an electronic signature that fulfils the required functions. Both assumptions are worth dwelling on.

---

[64] Kamerstukken I 2002/03, 27 743, No. 35, pp. 9-10.

The first assumption concerns the following: an electronic signature can perform a certain function, but a technical means other than an electronic signature may be more suitable to perform the function. The cautionary function is a case in point. An electronic signature may fulfil the cautionary function. A signatory may very well be aware of what he is doing when he is attaching his electronic signature to an electronic document. At the same time, it seems to me that the awareness of performing a legal act is to an even greater extent determined by the layout of the user interface of the software for conducting transactions. The user interface can clarify through visual aids, through explanatory text, through explicit warnings, exactly when as well as that a legal act is about to be performed. Given this example, it is clear that it must not always be the electronic signature that performs traditional signature functions. So, with respect to form requirements where, e.g., the cautionary function is relevant, one has to consider whether the rationale of the form requirement cannot be realised through means other than an electronic signature. Directive 2000/31/EC goes some way in requiring that a service provider makes available to the recipient of the service, effective and accessible technical means allowing him to identify and correct input errors, prior to the placing of the order (Article 11 paragraph 2 Directive 2000/31/EC). The provision thus requires that the technical make-up of the user-interface is such that a 'recipient of the service' can discern whether or not the order has been placed.

In general one can say that additional measures are required if functions can be better performed on-line by technological measures other than electronic signatures. This can be done by introducing new requirements that make the function(s) explicit.

Sometimes a function cannot be performed at all with the help of an electronic signature. The function of originality is a case in point. Originality refers to the state of not being a copy. In the traditional 'paper' environment, originality can, generally, easily be detected, since it is difficult to create an exact replica of a paper document. Copies made with the use of generally available copying techniques (such as photocopying) often show clear quality differences with the original. With respect to digital data, it is not clear how 'originality' could be defined and even whether 'originality' should be defined. Perhaps one could define the original as the first set of digital data that came into being. Later replicas of digital data are, however, not distinguishable from the 'original'. Therefore, this concept of originality seems less suitable for use in practice, unless additional measures are taken in order to make the 'originality' perceptible. Timestamping could be such a measure; it may not remove all questions, however.

The main functions of originality under the law are twofold:
- Originality has an evidentiary dimension to it. Originality is seen as a token of the authenticity of a document and thus adds to its evidentiary value. The Dutch private instrument and authentic deed, for example, enjoy their special evidentiary status only if they are originals. There are a few exceptions to this rule, but they will not be dealt with here.
- Original documents can be used as documents of title, such as bills of lading. It is the uniqueness of original documents that makes them suitable for such use. A carrier will, for example, deliver the goods to the person that is able to surrender an original bill of lading. Since a cargo can be delivered only once, it is important that not too many documents circulate that can pass off as original bills of lading.

The evidentiary function
Since originality is undefined or not very useable with respect to digital documents, the special evidentiary value which the law denotes to original paper documents does not apply to digital documents. The fact that originality is not a means for heightening the evidentiary value of digital documents, does of course not detract from the fact that the reliability of such documents can be enlarged by other means, such as the use of (asymmetric) encryption, good logging practices, the use of WORM media, etc. The use of such technologies may convince a judge or other arbitrator of the evidentiary value that can be attached to such means of evidence. For the time being, statutory law denotes a fixed evidentiary value to the use of such technologies only to a limited extent. The Directive on electronic signatures provides, for example, a special status to advanced electronic signatures, certified by a qualified certification authority. Such a careful approach on the part of the legislator is a wise move, given the little experience that exists with respect to technologies that heighten evidentiary value.

The function of 'uniqueness' pertaining to originality
This second function will here be illustrated with the aid of the bill of lading as an example, which may in practice be the most frequently occurring application of an original document as a document of title.

The three main functions of a bill of lading are the following:
- Receipt, the carrier hands the bill of lading to the shipper upon receiving the goods. The bill of lading confirms the receipt, it contains a description of the goods and the condition in which they are received.
- Contract of carriage, the bill of lading contains the carriage contract.
- Transfer of the possessory rights in the goods. This may also result in the title or property in the goods being transferred, if this is what is intended by the contract of sale. At the port of destination, the carrier will deliver the goods to the person who surrenders a bill of lading.

We deal here only with the bill of lading because of its third function, since this is illustrative with respect to originality. For those interested in other aspects of bills of lading, we refer to the traditional literature on the subject. As stated, an original bill of lading is an instrument for transferring the possessory rights in a cargo to a third party and the presentation of an original bill of lading is the means to obtain delivery of the goods. The carrier may only deliver the goods against the production of an original bill of lading. He may thus not deliver the cargo without any bill of lading being produced, or against a copy. This protects the shipper or subsequent owner of the cargo against the insolvency of the buyer; after all, the original bill of lading is only transferred after payment or against the provision of sufficient financial security.

As is apparent from the English case of *Motis* v. *Dampskibselskabet*, the requirement of the original bill of lading also serves to protect against fraud.[65] In this case, a carrier had delivered the goods to the holder of a forged bill of lading. Although the forgery was not apparent, the carrier was held liable for the loss suffered by the holder of the original bill of lading. The decision was appealed, but the court of appeal upheld the decision of the Commercial court:[66]

---

[65] See *Motis Exports* v. *Dampskibselskabet AF* 1912 [1999] 1 Lloyd's Rep. 837.
[66] See *Motis Exports* v. *Dampskibselskabet AF* 1912 [2000] 1 Lloyd's Rep. 211.

'20. In my judgment Mr Justice Rix was correct to characterize what occurred as misdelivery. A forged bill of lading is in the eyes of the law a nullity; it is simply a piece of paper with writing on it, which has no effect whatever. That being so delivery of the goods, or in this case the delivery order which was tantamount to the delivery of the goods, was not in exchange for the original bill of lading but for a worthless piece of paper'.

The carrier may thus be very well advised to inspect a surrendered bill of lading in order to determine whether it is genuine or a forgery.

The use of paper bills of lading does however entail important disadvantages. It is not uncommon, for example, that a cargo arrives at the port of destination before the bill of lading does. In order to be able to unload the vessel, the carrier is usually prepared to do so against a letter of indemnity. This is no more than a makeshift measure, however. This drawback can be counteracted by digitalizing the functions of the traditional paper bill of lading and the processes of handling it.

From a legal perspective, such a digitalization project encounters two main problems.

In the first place, there is insecurity with respect to the applicability of existing legislation concerning bills of lading or, more generally, documents of title, since existing law contains traditional terminology, such as 'document', 'writing' and 'signature'. The existing statutory law can be found in international conventions, such as the Hague-Visby Rules and the Hamburg Rules or the Convention for the Unification of Certain Rules relating to Bills of Lading, signed at Brussels on 25th August 1924 (including Amending Protocols). Furthermore, such law can be found in national statutes, such as The Carriage of Goods by Sea Act of 1992 (in the UK) or Book 8 of the Dutch Civil Code (hereinafter: DCC). Wording such as signature, writing or document renders their applicability to electronic bills of lading unsure.

In the second place, there can be some doubt about the suitability of electronic messages as a means to perform the traditional function of bills of lading, because of the differing physical characteristics of electronic messages as compared to paper documents. The supposed characteristic of paper documents that exists in the fact that originals can be distinguished from copies means that original paper documents are recognizably unique: a copy is recognized as such (at least that is the commonly used presumption). This uniqueness of original paper documents is however only relative: in practice, often more than one original is drawn up. That is no problem, as long as the paper documents do not fall into the hands of persons who may not have the documents at their disposal. The singular characteristic of a paper document facilitates that the disposition over documents can be held to be exclusive. Digital data, on the other hand, are multiple. The transfer of digital data to a receiver does not imply that the sender no longer possesses the data. This characteristic could entail that something like an 'electronic bills of lading' becomes more widely dispersed than is desirable. The relative uniqueness that is part and parcel of 'original' documents is not present with documents or messages that contain digital data.

The doubt about the physical suitability may even reinforce insecurity with respect to the applicability of statutory provisions mentioned previously. The doubt concerning the physical suitability may however be removed or lessened by building more security into the processes used to handle 'electronic bills of lading'. Hereinafter, we will see that Bolero directs all messages through a central messaging platform, thus enabling various kinds of checks.

The problem with respect to the applicability of the statutory provisions may be solved in two alternative or cumulative ways:

1. It is conceivable that existing legislation will be adapted. UNCITRAL's Working Group on electronic commerce has done a great deal of work in this respect.
2. The same functionalities may be performed while making use of other legal concepts and constructions. The legal forms may then be chosen in such a way that national and international legislation do not constitute an obstacle. Hereinafter, we will see that Bolero has brought all processes with respect to its 'Bolero Bill of Lading' (hereinafter: BBL) into a contractual framework that functions as a layer that somewhat isolates the BBL from national and international legislation.

Ad 1
The UNCITRAL model law on electronic commerce contains two articles on transport documentation; its scope is thus somewhat wider than bills of

lading alone.[67] The core provision can be found in Article 17 section 3. It reads as follows:

> '(3) If a right is to be granted to, or an obligation is to be acquired by, one person and no other person, and if the law requires that, in order to effect this, the right or obligation must be conveyed to that person by the transfer, or use of, a paper document, that requirement is met if the right or obligation is conveyed by using one or more data messages, provided that a reliable method is used to render such data message or messages unique'.

Note that the place of a paper document can be taken by one or more data messages. It is however not required that one of these messages takes the place of 'the' paper document or that it is 'the' electronic bill of lading. The messages need also not be unique in themselves, but they may derive their uniqueness from the procedure in which they are used. The model law thus leaves some room to adapt the processes surrounding transport documentation to the characteristic traits of ICT.

The method that renders the messages unique must be reliable. This reliability is to be assessed in the light of the purpose for which the right or obligation was conveyed and in the light of all circumstances, including any relevant agreement (section 4).

Ad 2

The use of legal concepts and constructions other than 'bill of lading' can be illustrated with the help of Bolero.

> 'Bolero is not the first initiative to take bills of lading to the digital environment.[68] Previous initiatives include the CMI Rules and SeaDocs. We confine ourselves to the Bolero since it seems to be the most viable of initiatives. Other initiatives, such as Trade Card, are not dealt with either'.

All parties involved enter into contractual relations with Bolero International Ltd. and Bolero Association Ltd. The latter agreement is accompanied by the Bolero Rule Book and operational procedures. All electronic communications are encrypted using public key encryption. The contrac-

---

[67] Clift 1999.
[68] See Burnett 2001, Laryea 2001 and Faber 1996.

tual agreements lay the basis for the legal validity of the communications. Communications do not take place directly from party to party, but involve the title registry, which is thus in a central position allowing it to keep an eye on 'uniqueness'.

As an illustration, a possible trace of a Bolero Bill of Lading is described here:

When receiving a cargo, the carrier creates a so-called Bolero Bill of Lading (hereinafter: BBL). The BBL is an electronic document containing the same information as a traditional bill of lading. The carrier sends the BBL to Bolero International's title registry. The title registry checks the digital signature of the carrier, registers the BBL in the registry and passes the BBL on to the shipper. If the shipper or a subsequent holder of the BBL wishes to transfer the cargo while at sea, he passes the BBL on to the transferee and notifies the registry. Upon notification, the title of the current holder is cancelled and the title is transferred to the next holder. The new holder has 24 hours to inform the registry that he accepts that he is the new holder. Legally, a new carriage agreement between the new holder and carrier arises through novation. At the same time, Bolero International informs the new holder on behalf of the carrier that the latter holds the goods to the new holder's order. Legally, this constitutes attornment.

When the goods arrive at the port of destination, the holder surrenders his BBL to Bolero International. Bolero International notifies the carrier of the surrender and confirms the surrender to the 'holder'. The 'holder' can collect the goods at the port of destination upon identification as required by the carrier or the port.

We see that every communication involves Bolero International. It checks the digital signatures of the messages it receives and checks the contents of the messages against the title registry. It is through the procedures employed (and not the electronic messages per se) that the uniqueness of the 'holder' is guaranteed. In the context of bills of lading 'originality' is thus reduced to its core element. The uniqueness is guaranteed in a way that fits in with the special characteristics of ICT.

Conclusion
In general, it is a good approach to qualify an electronic signature as a 'signature' if it is functionally equivalent. The off-line model lends itself well to transposition to the on-line environment. In certain special cases,

the extrapolation of the signature model to the on-line environment is however inadequate. In such cases, a broader approach is necessary and desirable. Other technologies must be called upon to fulfil certain functions that are traditionally performed by signatures. Only by broadening the approach, can one fully employ the potential of ICT.

3.3   EVIDENTIARY VALUE

If a party is involved in a dispute and comes to rely on an electronic signature, the question arises what evidentiary value a court attributes to the electronic signature. Since electronic signatures are a relatively new technology, uncertainty concerning the answer to this question is bound to exist. Does Directive 1999/93/EC help? Directive 1999/93/EC states that advanced electronic signatures, based on a qualified certificate, must be admissible in evidence. A 'normal' electronic signature may not be denied admissibility solely on the ground that it is in electronic form or misses out on certain aspects of advanced signatures, based on qualified certificates.

The admissibility issue need not be implemented in Dutch law. According to Dutch law, evidence can be adduced by every means. The evaluation of the evidentiary value is left to the court.[69] A court is only restrained in the sense that clearly incorrect assessments may impair its authority. The principle that the assessment of the evidentiary value is left to the judgement of the court is not detracted from in favour of (electronic) signatures.[70] It may therefore seem that Directive 1999/93/EC does not have an added effect. This may, however, not be completely true. The directive cannot be read otherwise than that advanced signatures based on a qualified certificate are considered to be trustworthy electronic signatures. With respect to other electronic signatures the directive signals that they may very well contribute to the proof of facts. In this sense, the directive has a symbolic value in that it points to direction in which developments may proceed. It is a first step in the direction of a

---

[69] See Art. 152 DCCP.

[70] That is, apart from the minor restriction in a court's discretion that it may not deny every evidentiary value purely because the signature is electronic in nature.

more ready acceptance of electronic signatures as evidence. In dealing with electronic signatures in the way in which the directive does, it gives a signal that a court perhaps may not wish to ignore completely. Relying parties can, however, not be given any guarantee: a court remains free in its assessment of the evidentiary value it is willing to attribute to electronic signatures. For relying parties, the directive is a symbolic step in the right direction, but caselaw has to be awaited for assurance.

Comparison with traditional signatures
Dutch civil law does not provide special rules with respect to the evidentiary value of signed documents. However, if a document is a private instrument, the Dutch Code of Civil Procedure stipulates that the private instrument provides compulsory proof between the parties of the truth of the party declarations which it contains. This means that a court is bound to accept the truth of the party statements contained in the private instrument; the court may not assess the evidentiary value itself. It can, however, allow another party to prove that the contents cannot be accepted as true.

Apart from proof of the truth of its contents, a private instrument may also provide proof of the identity of the signatory or signatories and proof of the integrity of the data in the document. The DCCP does however not provide special rules concerning the evidentiary value of these aspects of a private instrument. This means that a court is free in its assessment of the private instrument with respect to these probanda.

Given the fact that the Dutch Code of Civil Procedure binds special legal consequences to the qualifiability of a document as a private instrument, one could ask whether a signed electronic document can be considered to be a private instrument. A private instrument is a signed written document, meant as proof. Thus, apart from a signature, also the writing and the evidentiary purpose are requirements. For those 'extra' requirements, one can ask whether they, too, can be fulfilled by electronic means. For a requirement that is not technology-dependent, such as the evidentiary purpose, this may not pose too great a problem. The requirement of a written document, on the other hand, is technology-dependent and may therefore not be fulfilled when using electronic means. Can an electronic document qualify as a written document? In this case, we do not have to start from zero, but we can follow on from the directive on electronic commerce. Article 9 section 1 Directive 2000/31/EC states that

Member States shall ensure that their legal system allows contracts to be concluded by electronic means. Member States shall in particular ensure that the legal requirements applicable to the contractual process neither create obstacles for the use of electronic contracts nor result in such contracts being deprived of legal effectiveness and validity on account of their having been made by electronic means.

The Dutch Electronic Signatures Act describes with what requirements a functional digital equivalent of a written document must comply (Article 6: 227a DCC). According to the proposal, an electronic document can be put on a par with a written document, if it meets four requirements, that is to say: if it is readable by the parties, if the authenticity of the contract is sufficiently guaranteed, if the moment of the materialisation of the contract can be determined with sufficient certainty and if the identities of the parties can be determined with sufficient certainty. The requirements concerning the identities of the parties and the authenticity of the contract can in my view be met by using a suitable electronic signature. This is underlined by Directive 1999/93/EC in that it demands like requirements for an advanced electronic signature: the advanced electronic signature must be capable of identifying the signatory and it must be linked to the data to which it relates in such a manner that any subsequent change of the data is detectable (Article 2 sub. 2 Directive 1999/93/EC). That leaves only the two remaining requirements to be met. The moment of the contract's materialisation can be ascertained with the help of a timestamping service. The readability of the contract is also matter of choosing appropriate technologies.

The remaining question is whether having functional equivalents of the components of a private instrument (signed and in writing) also means that the resulting signed electronic document can be qualified as a private instrument. According to the Dutch government, this will indeed be the case, once the statute implementing Directive 2000/31/EC has been implemented in Dutch law. The Act implementing Directive 1999/93/EC has received Royal Assent in May 2003. In the preparatory documents to the statute implementing Directive 1999/93/EC the government stated the following (in unofficial translation):[71]

---

[71] Kamerstukken I 2002/2003, 27 743, No. 35 (MvA), p. 10.

'Within the boundaries of Arts. 3:15a and 6:227a DCC it will indeed be possible to comply with the signature and writing requirements for an instrument.
A status equal to an instrument, therefore stands to reason [...]'.

This result is not incompatible with what had earlier been advocated in the
literature.[72]

One relativation with regard to positive law must be made, however.
The functional equivalent of a written document only relates to contracts.
A private instrument can however be used for legal acts other than just
contracts. For these other legal acts, the status of an electronic document
(in writing or not?) is still uncertain.

In the context of substantive law, an electronic document that meets
the requirements of Article 3:15a DCC (on electronic signatures) and Article 6:227a DCC (on being in writing) can thus be considered to be a private instrument. Does this mean that such an electronic document is also
a private instrument for the purpose of the law of evidence? This question
must be answered in the affirmative; even more so, because substantive
law relies on the definition of a private instrument as given in the DCCP.
The government considers such an electronic document also to be a private instrument for evidentiary purposes.[73] However, private instruments
only enjoy their special evidentiary authority if they are originals; copies
are merely 'ordinary' writing (Article 160 section 1 DCCP). It is still not
yet completely clear what requirements an electronic document must
meet for it to be the functional equivalent of a paper original. The government does not specifically address the question of originality and simply
states that an electronic document that can be equated with a private instrument has the same coercive evidentiary authority as a paper private
instrument. If one takes this statement as a starting point, this might mean
that the form requirement of originality no longer applies with respect to
electronic documents, as far as the law of evidence is concerned! This
may be too drastic a conclusion, however. Traditionally, originality functions in an evidentiary setting as a token of authenticity and integrity. It is
not plausible that the functions of authenticity and integrity are no longer

---

[72] See Kemna 2001, p. 172 and Van Esch 1999.
[73] Kamerstukken I 2002/2003, 27 743, No. 35 (MvA), p. 10.

of value with respect to electronic documents. However, with respect to private instruments it may very well be advocated that the requirement of originality does not 'add' anything. The requirements of Articles 3:15a DCC and 6:227a DCC together may very well be considered to be a sufficient guarantee of authenticity, thus making an extra requirement of 'originality' superfluous with respect to 'electronic' private instruments.

It goes without saying that parties can take responsibility themselves to ameliorate the evidentiary value of electronic signatures with the help of technical and contractual measures. They may agree about the evidentiary value which electronic signatures have in their mutual relations, unless by doing so they would dispose of rights which they cannot dispose of (see Article 153 DCCP). The choice of suitable authentication technologies can also serve to lessen the risk of a court attributing little or no evidentiary value to an electronic signature.

Conclusion concerning evidentiary aspects
In principle a court is free to attribute to an electronic signature and the document with which it is associated any evidentiary value it thinks fit. Directive 1999/93/EC does not, and must not, remove this discretion from the courts. The discretion is too much a cornerstone of the Dutch law of evidence. The contribution of the directive must rather be sought in the fact that it has a symbolic value: it may change the perception of the reliability of electronic signatures. When such a change in perception will occur is however difficult to predict.

The implementation of the directive does bring something new to Dutch law: a signed electronic document may be qualified as a private instrument; the coercive evidentiary authority with respect to the truth of the party declarations may therefore also be invoked with respect to such electronic documents. A 'drawback' remains that for a document to qualify as a private instrument, it must meet the requirements for functional equivalence. This means, for example, that the signature must be sufficiently reliable as a method of authentication. This requirement thus brings about the possibility again to raise doubts as to the reliability of electronic signatures. There seems to be no way around this problem, however. Trust in electronic signatures must grow through use. It cannot be commandeered, not even by the legislator.

3.4   SEMI-LEGAL CONSIDERATIONS OF USABILITY

Apart from the strictly legal aspect of usability (which is the subject of this chapter) there is another, wider framework, in which a person, company or organisation will place the usability of an electronic signature, before it may decide that electronic signatures are to be used. This wider framework will only be described in its main features and not in extenso; the aim is merely to indicate within which wider context the strictly legal considerations in this chapter must be placed. It will be assumed that a person, company or other organisation seeks trust and security in the use of electronic signatures; this will be elaborated hereinafter. The assessment that must subsequently be made is whether the electronic signature is indeed in the concrete reality of that person, company or organisation the most suitable means to realise that goal.[74] In the context of this assessment several considerations will play a role: considerations concerning proportionality (what level of trust and security are required in concreto?), considerations of subsidiarity (what alternatives to electronic signatures exist?) and considerations of cost-efficiency (do the benefits exceed the costs?). These elements will be succinctly dealt with here.

Trust
A signature conveys no or at least very little information about the signatory, apart from his identity. From a signature, viewed as data alone, one cannot derive direct information about the trustworthiness of the signatory. Nonetheless, a signature has an important role in conveying trust. The trust that signatures inspire stems from the meaning that society binds to signatures and the act of signing. A signature is a means to express the seriousness of one's intentions. The signatory binds himself irreversibly to the contents of the signed document. Repudiation of the signature at a later point in time is difficult if not practically impossible. The signatory binds his name to the contents of the signed document. He sacrifices the possibility or freedom to distance himself from the document at a later point in time. The fact that the signatory is willing to bind himself, to commit himself in a generally accepted and therefore irreversible manner is a source of

---

[74] See also Winn 2001.

trust for the relying party. The signature and the trust that stems therefrom, is a sound and generally recognised basis upon which to act. Being able to build upon signed statements is an important facilitator for various kinds of activities. Being able to trust, acts as a lubricant that makes many societal activities run more smoothly and efficiently than would ever be possible without such trust. It also reduces the cost of certain activities as expensive checks may be omitted.

Security
If something goes wrong the signature is a form of security. The security that signatures provide is somehow a logic extension of the fact that society places trust in signatures. The law 'recognises' the trust that society places in signatures. It does so by considering signed statements as statements which bind the signatory. Moreover, the law provides the means to enforce the obligations that stem from the signed statements.

An electronic signature is a good potential means for bringing about trust and security. Whether this potential can be realised in a concrete setting of a signature user – such as a person, company or organisation – requires an assessment of considerations about proportionality, subsidiarity and cost-efficiency as we saw above.

Proportionality
Also the need for trust and security – and in its wake the need for electronic signatures as a means for achieving them – must sometimes be critically appraised. A business model may, for example, be set up in such a way that one does not need to, or to a much lesser extent, trust one's transacting partner. A lesser need for trust may come about in the following situation. An e-business may, for instance, require that a consumer pays in advance. As the e-business incurs no or little risk, it does not need to trust the consumer. It must however be said that trustless business misses out on the advantages that business based on trust thrives upon. The 'lubricant' function of trust that was mentioned above may have the same beneficial influence for e-commerce as it has on off-line business. A trustless e-business may therefore always be somewhat hampered.

Security may also not be required, or to a much lesser extent than one would 'normally' expect. This may be the case, for example, with small value transactions. The (small) value of a transaction may not warrant that much is invested in 'security'. It may be more economical to lose money on some transactions than to spend a great deal on security in the form of electronic signatures.

Subsidiarity
Trust and security may be gained through means other than electronic signatures.

Trust and security are desirable commodities, but it need not be an electronic signature that brings them about. There are many alternative sources of trust and security. Trust in a party may be gained, for example, by consulting a third party or by building on the reputation of the envisaged contracting partner. In this respect, the registers kept by chambers of commerce and certification schemes, such as webtrader, perform a useful function. A famous trademark or trade name may inspire trust as well.

Trust can also be won from positive previous business experiences. Sometimes, it is possible to build upon an existing relationship. Such a relationship may even originate in the off-line world. Negative previous experience may be registered in a blacklist. Although, this may have serious privacy implications for the persons who are registered, it is an effective means to exclude certain bad 'risks'.

Furthermore, parties taking part in e-commerce may take precautionary measures in order to heighten trust and security. Trust and security may be gained by setting up e-business in such a way that misunderstandings and intentional sabotage are excluded as far as is possible. The make-up of a web site may, for example, be formed in such a way that mistakes are prevented as far as possible. Communication from and to a web site can be secured through a Secure Socket Layer. An SSL is a form of communications security and not so much a signature, since the identification of the 'author' of messages and endorsement/authentication by that author is lacking. On-line communications may be verified with the help of traditional means; think of verification by telephone. Last but not least, insurance may offer security (or at least financial compensation) against untrustworthy contracting partners.

The examples mentioned serve to illustrate that trust and security may be gained through a wide variety of means. These means may remove the need for electronic signatures, or at least lessen the need for electronic signatures.

Benefits and cost

The adequacy of electronic signatures for providing trust is limited. A signature merely indicates an identity and provides authentication. Knowing somebody's identity and having him authenticate a document does not however guarantee that he is reliable as a business partner. This may require additional measures.

Electronic signatures do not come without cost. This holds even more true for electronic signatures that involve trusted third parties. The users of electronic signatures may, for example, have to pay the TTP for services rendered and to cover the costs of liability. The maintenance of certificates is laborious and difficult to keep up to date. Furthermore, a party taking the initiative to set up a PKI must make large investments. The cost and complicated nature of digital signatures may however be reduced by a simpler layout: a company or organisation may use electronic signatures only within existing relations with customers. If it builds on pre-existing infrastructure and investment, complexity and costs can be reduced: there is no TTP which has to certify data, the company or organisation is its own TTP.

Chapter 4
MISUSE AND THE BURDEN OF PROOF

Chapter 4
MISUSE AND THE BURDEN OF PROOF

4.1 INTRODUCTION

The usability of authentication technology depends, in the first place, on its recognition as a signature and its evidentiary value. These issues have been covered in the previous chapter. Usability is however also determined by more secondary concerns, such as certainty with respect to what will occur when an electronic signature is abused. In order to shed some light on this question, two connected issues are addressed in this chapter: on the one hand, the liability for unauthorised use of an electronic signature and, on the other, the division of the burden of proof if a dispute arises as to the signature or the document to which it is attached.

4.2 THE DIVISION OF RISKS

Many issues surrounding liability with respect to an electronic signature may be discerned. Since the focus of this book is on electronic signatures, one liability issue will be further investigated that is closely connected with the use of electronic signatures and perhaps less so with the electronic documents they are contained in: the liability flowing from unauthorised use of an electronic signature. In order to structure the discussion, the following general case is taken as a starting point: suppose a third party succeeds in using, without authority, the electronic signature that belongs to somebody else (the holder). He uses the electronic signature to perform a legal act that involves another party: the relying party, e.g., the third party concludes a contract with the relying party. From this use, the relying party or the holder suffers damage. Furthermore, it is assumed that no compensation can be obtained from the third party, since it or its assets cannot be traced. That

M.H.M. Schellekens, Electronic Signatures
© *2004, ITeR, The Hague, and the author*

raises the following question: who has to bear the loss? Three parties are candidates: the holder of the electronic signature, the relying party and, *casu quo*, the certification authority.

The liability of the certification authority
The behaviour of the certification authority may be a cause that contributes to the unauthorised use of the electronic signature in various ways. It is, for example, possible that the certification authority (or perhaps better: the registering authority) did not sufficiently check the identity of a person requesting the certificate, thus allowing this person to obtain a certificate by claiming the identity of somebody else. Another example may be that the certification authority, having received notification of the compromise of a private key, takes too much time to bring about a revocation, thus enabling the third party to use the electronic signature in the meantime. According to recital 22 of Directive 1999/93/EC, the liability of the certification authority, providing services to the public, must be dealt with under the normal national rules regarding liability. For Dutch law this means with fault liability under contract law (e.g., on the basis of the CPS) or as an unlawful act. Article 6 Directive 1999/93/EC provides some specific rules on the liability of a certification service provider (hereinafter: CSP) issuing a certificate as a qualified certificate to the public or guaranteeing such certificate to the public. Such a CSP is liable for damage caused to a person who reasonably relies on the certificate:

• as regards the accuracy at the time of issuing of all information contained in the qualified certificate and as regards the fact that the certificate contains all the details prescribed for a qualified certificate;
• for assurance that at the time of the issuing of the certificate, the signatory identified in the qualified certificate held the signature-creation data corresponding to the signature-verification data given or identified in the certificate;
• for assurance that the signature-creation data and the signature-verification data can be used in a complementary manner in cases where the certification service-provider generates them both;
• for failure to register the revocation of the certificate.

The certification service-provider can free himself from liability by proving that he has not acted negligently. The person suffering damage is thus assisted by a reversal of the burden of proof with respect to negligence on the part of the CSP.

The holder and the relying party
The division of the risks between the holder and the relying party is closely connected to the question whether the holder is bound by the legal act, such as the contract, that the unauthorised party sought to bring about. Resolving the question of the binding nature is a necessary condition for answering the question of the division of risks. This raises the question of what in general is the basis for becoming bound to a legal act. In Dutch law, a legal act requires the intent to bring about a legal effect, an intent which is revealed through a declaration (Article 3:33 Dutch Civil Code). Like many other continental European countries, Dutch law thus chooses a subjective approach. It is the inner intent that is the basis for being bound to a legal act. The declaration of intent is 'merely' a necessary condition to make the intent cognisable to other persons.

In contrast, under English law, the declaration and the reasonable reliance of another party on that declaration are more important than intent. Atiyah formulates this as follows:[75]

'Every law student is taught from his earliest days that contractual intent is not really what it seems; actual subjective intent is normally irrelevant. It is the appearance, the manifestation of intent that matters. Whenever a person is held bound by a promise or a contract contrary to his actual intent or understanding, it is plain that liability is based not on some notion of a voluntary assumption of obligation, but on something else. And most frequently it will be found that that something else is the element of reasonable reliance'.

---

[75] Atiyah 1986, p. 21. See also Atiyah 1981, p. 6: 'It is one of the most fundamental features of the law of contract that the test of agreement is objective and not subjective. In other words, it matters not whether the parties have really agreed in their innermost minds. The question is not whether the parties have really agreed, but whether their conduct and language are such as would lead reasonable people to assume that they have agreed'. See also Weitzenboeck 2001.

This raises the question whether or not in Dutch law something like 'reasonable reliance' actually plays no role at all. To answer this question, one has to investigate the situation under Dutch law if, for whatever cause, somebody's declaration (or something that seems to be somebody's declaration) does not correspond to his intention. It appears that, in such cases, Dutch law does not unreservedly adhere to its starting point that the inner will is determinative. The reliance of a party on a declaration or the semblance of a declaration can be the basis for binding the person who declares or seems to declare. The trust that a party places in another's declaration, while it does not know and does not need to know that a corresponding will is lacking, is thus sometimes honoured and the person who seems to declare is bound to something beyond his will. The question is in what circumstances is such a reliance honoured and can take the place of the lacking intent. Here, the discussion will focus on the case when an unauthorised party has signed a declaration with the holder's electronic signature and that therefore the semblance of a declaration by the holder is created towards the relying party. In such a case, the holder of the electronic signature will want to state that the signature does not bind him, since it does not originate from him. The relying party will want to state that it may trust an electronic signature, of which it does not know better and need not know better than that it has been placed by its legitimate holder. In order to investigate this issue, two judgements of the Dutch Supreme Court – hereinafter: the Hoge Raad (HR) – are presented. The first case involves a forgery of a traditional handwritten signature; the second involves the unauthorised use of an electronic signature.

The judgement in HR 7 February 1992 NJ 1992, 809, RvdW 1992, 46 (Kamerman/Aro) sheds some light on the division of risks in the case of forgery.

In an unofficial translation, the main consideration of the judgement reads as follows:

> 'When somebody, by fraudulently placing somebody else's signature, declares something for that other person, this person can invoke against the person to whom the declaration was directed, that the signature and thereby the declaration do not originate from him, even if the person to whom the declaration was directed assumed and reasonably could assume that the signature was authentic.

From the principle that underlies Articles 3.35, 3:36 and 3:61 section 2 DCC, in conjunction with Article 6:147 DCC it follows however ... that this may be otherwise in special circumstances. These circumstances must be such that they impose the conclusion that it can be imputed to the person whose signature has been forged that the opposing party considered and reasonably could consider that the signature was authentic. This may, for example, be the case when the person whose signature has been forged, although he knew or ought to have known of the untrustworthiness of the person who forged his signature, has lent his co-operation to, or without precautions has allowed that person – by forging his signature – to have the opportunity to create the appearance that it concerned a declaration that was signed by him'.

With respect to the unauthorised use of an electronic signature, the following applies, as is apparent from the COVA case.[76]

'The question which of the parties, in the absence of a contractual agreement in this respect, ought to bear the risk of abuse of an agreed code, must be answered on the basis of the concrete circumstances of the case, taking into account that it is of special importance to whom it can be imputed that the unauthorised person obtained knowledge of the code. If the unauthorised person is employed by the client [i.e., the holder of the code with which the electronic signature can be created (M.S.)] or if he otherwise has a certain relationship with the client that places him in a position in which he, more easily than random third persons, could have access to the code, then there will in general be reason for such an imputation to the client, because in principle it can be assumed that the misuse is attributable to his lack of care. This may only be otherwise in circumstances that exclude such a lack of care. It is up to the client to raise and prove such circumstances'.

Whether the trust that a relying party places in an electronic signature is honoured, depends on whom it can be imputed that the unauthorised person obtained the code. In the first place, acquiring the code may be imputable to the relying party. This could arguably be the case where symmetric encryption is used and the unauthorised party has wormed the key out of the relying party. Often, however, the question of imputability to the relying party may demonstrate an overlap with the question whether the relying party reasonably relied on the signature. Once it appears that the relying

---

[76] HR 19 November 1993, NJ 1994, 622, RvdW 1993, 230 (COVA/NMB).

party could not reasonably rely on the signature, the question of imputability does not arise. It may also appear that the loss of the exclusivity of the code is imputable to the holder. The holder may, for example, have acted negligently with respect to the means for bringing about the signature, such as the private key or his PIN, thus allowing the third party to avail himself of the means. Often the discussion will focus on the imputability to the holder. What can be learned from the above judgements about the conditions under which an appearance of authenticity, casu quo authorised use, can be imputed to the holder? Are the conditions for imputation in case of an unauthorised use of an electronic signature the same as the conditions in the case of a forgery of a traditional handwritten signature? In order to answer this question, first the relevant technical differences have to be determined. The main difference often referred to is that a traditional signature is a personal creation, whereas the electronic signature is an artefact that can in principle be reproduced by everybody. What legal relevance can this technical difference have? The following arguments could be raised:

- Using an electronic signature without authority is easier than forging a traditional signature, which requires some skill. The risk of abuse of an electronic signature is greater.
- In the case of an electronic signature, the relying party cannot verify the authority to use, since the unauthorised person uses the authentic signature.
- The holder of an electronic signature has to take precautionary measures to prevent abuse. The holder of a traditional signature can hardly take precautionary measures, since such a signature is necessarily less or more public. One cannot use one's traditional signature without showing it to other people.

The first two arguments must however be strictly made relative.

- Forging a traditional signature is not so difficult, because a traditional signature is less or more public; forgers may thus experience little trouble in finding a copy of a signature that can serve as a template for the forgery. The means to forge a signature (pen and paper) are widely available and a forgery need not be an exact replica, since the authentic signature itself may change over time.

- In the case of an electronic signature, a relying party can easily make verifications, such as checking CRLs, whereas the verification of traditional signatures may very well be far from perfect, since the verification is usually performed by laymen.

The third argument (concerning precautionary measures) could perhaps also be made relative in that the Kamerman decision shows that also the holder of a traditional signature may have to tread carefully, because he may under certain circumstances act so negligently that he must accept that the law protects the reliance of another party on a forgery of his signature. However, when comparing both decisions with respect to the care which a holder has to exercise, it becomes clear that the imputation in the case of a forgery of a traditional handwritten signature requires more compelling circumstances than in the case of an unauthorised use of an electronic signature. In the case of an electronic signature, the mere creation of an opportunity for an unauthorised person to make use of that signature is enough to impute the semblance of authorised use to the holder. Placing somebody in a position in which he – more easily than random others – can use the electronic signature (thus creating an opportunity) was enough for such an imputation in the COVA case. With respect to a traditional handwritten signature, the mere creation of an opportunity to forge the signature is insufficient. There must be additional circumstances that make the creation of opportunity so negligent that it can be imputed. In the Kamerman case, it was not enough that Kamerman (the holder of a handwritten signature) registered her friend's business in her name (thus creating the opportunity), it also had to be established that she knew or ought to have known that her friend was unreliable (making the creation of the opportunity negligent).

With respect to a traditional signature, hardly any precautionary measures can be taken against forgery. Measures that cannot be taken, of course, need not be taken. With respect to an electronic signature, precautionary measures against unauthorised use can very well be taken and, consequently, they must be taken. Failing to do so, provides a strong argument for the imputation of a semblance of authorised use to the holder. However, the fact that in the case of an electronic signature measures can be taken may prove to be technology dependent. If an electronic signature is secured with the help of biometric technologies, the user may again find himself in the situation that he can hardly take any precautionary measures: what specific measures could one take to protect one's finger-print?

All in all, if one is to compare the division of the risks in the case of an electronic signature to that in the case of a forged traditional signature, the following marked differences can be noted:

- The apparent basic position of the Hoge Raad in the COVA case has been met by criticism; in the literature, it is contended that it does not do enough to stimulate trust in commercial dealings, since it is the re-lying party that has to prove that it can be imputed to the holder that the unauthorised party obtained the means to create the signature.[77] The position that 'a relying party must be able to trust' seems to be rather commonplace.[78]
- The Hoge Raad found in both cases some degree of negligence on the part of the holder and used this as a basis for imputing the (semblance of a) declaration to the holder. In the context of Article 3:35 Dutch Civil Code, it is sufficient that the appearance of a declaration is aroused by the person who may become bound without intent, it is not relevant whether he can be blamed for the appearance coming into existence.[79]
- In case of an electronic signature, the mere creation of an opportunity to abuse the electronic signature seems to be enough for imputing the appearance of authorised use to the holder, whereas in the case of a traditional signature, additional circumstances are required for mak-ing the creation of opportunity negligent.
- The extent and nature of the precautionary measures which a holder has to take are dependent upon the technology that is used. A tech-nology involving personal traits generally seems to 'require' less pre-cautionary measures than a technology based on something one knows (such as a PIN number) or something one has (such as a card).

---

[77] Van Esch 1999, pp. 161-164.

[78] See Art. 13 UNCITRAL Model law on Electronic Commerce 1996. According to Storme, the trust of the relying party is taken as the basic starting point under Belgian law. See Storme 2001, p. 1018.

[79] Hartkamp 2001, pp. 123-124.

- In the case of an unauthorised use of an electronic signature, the relying party is in certain cases assisted by a legal assumption of negligence on the part of the holder.

In practice, the division of risks will usually be the subject of a contractual agreement between the holder of the electronic signature and the relying party. In the case of electronic payment instruments, the European Commission has issued a recommendation concerning transactions by electronic payment instruments and in particular the relationship between the issuer and the holder.[80] This recommendation offers a guideline for banks in drawing up their contractual terms. The recommendation, *inter alia*, touches upon the subject of liability. According to Article 8 Recommendation 97/489/EC the issuer is liable for transactions that are not authorized by the holder. However, up to the time of notification, the holder bears the loss sustained as a consequence of the loss or theft of the electronic payment instrument up to a limit which may not exceed Euro 150, except where he has acted with extreme negligence, in contravention of certain obligations concerning the handling of the instrument, or has acted fraudulently, in which case such a limit does not apply. As soon as the holder has notified the issuer, he is not liable thereafter for the loss arising as a consequence of the loss or theft of his electronic payment instrument, except where he has acted fraudulently.

The governing principles, such as trust and (the absence of) the will to be bound, are not referred in the recommendation. Instead concrete circumstances and facts take their place, such as being notified (instead of the absence of trust), and concrete obligations concerning the handling of the payment instrument as a crystallisation of the possible reasons for imputing an appearance of authorised use. Parties may in this way enhance the legal certainty in their mutual relationship. The recommendation also deviates from the rules that are applicable in the absence of a contractual arrangement, e.g.: in case no party is to blame, a rudimentary division of the loss is recommended: the holder bears the first Euro 150, the bank the

---

[80] Commission Recommendation of 30 July 1997 concerning transactions by electronic payment instruments and in particular the relationship between issuer and holder, 97/489/EC, OJ L 208, 20/08/1997, pp. 0052-0058.

rest. The excess of Euro 150 may also serve as an incentive to notify a loss or theft of the payment instrument to the bank. Such a division of losses may very well not be the outcome that would be attained purely on the basis of objective Dutch law.

Conclusion

The issue of the division of risks in the case of an unauthorised use of an electronic signature is not completely resolved by Directive 1999/93/EC. Article 6 merely deals with the liability of certain certifying authorities. The division of risks between the holder of an electronic signature and the relying party is left unattended. This question has been dealt with according to Dutch law. From caselaw, it appears that there is a difference between traditional and electronic signatures with respect to the standard that is used to determine whether an appearance of authenticity or, as the case may be, authorised use of the signature can be imputed to the holder. In the case of an electronic signature (based on something one has, such as a card, and something one knows, such as a PIN code) the mere creation of circumstances in which an unauthorised use was possible is enough for such an imputation. If it concerns a traditional signature, additional circumstances are required. The mere creation of an opportunity is not enough for imputing a creation of appearance. Only additional circumstances point to the creation of opportunity being negligent. In short, it is dependent upon the technology what the nature and extent of the precautionary measures that rest on the holder are. As a consequence, the use of biometric technology can diminish the precautionary measures which a holder of an electronic signature has to take. It is therefore paramount that the holder is conscious of the implications which the choice of a certain technology entail. It also stresses the importance of the involvement of the (future) holders of electronic signatures in the process of setting up an infrastructure in which electronic signatures of a certain technology are to be used. It can be stated that the use of biometric technology thus contributes to legal certainty in two respects. On the one hand, it raises the threshold for imputability to the holder. On the other hand, it may diminish the number of cases in which an unauthorised person uses an electronic signature, because it is made more difficult.

4.3 THE DIVISION OF THE BURDEN OF PROOF

If somebody produces a document during proceedings as a means of evidence, the other party may object to the production of the document. He may for instance contend that the signature under the text is not his or that it has been forged or placed by a person who is not authorised to do so. He may also contend that the text of the document has been altered after signing, or he may contend that the statements contained in the document are not true, e.g., he did not have the capacity to accede to the agreement, he has been misled. If such a contention is sufficient to cast doubt on the evidentiary value of the document and the document is vital to the argumentation of one or more parties, one of the parties has to provide proof of her view. The question is which party has to produce proof of her view? If no special rules are applicable (and this is in principle the case with electronic documents), the main rule on the division of the burden of proof applies: he who invokes legal consequences relating to facts or rights he has asserted, has to prove those facts or rights (Article 150 DCCP). Applied to the situation of the document, this means that the party casting doubt about the document (typically the signatory or his legal successor) must prove the forgery, the unauthorised signing, the manipulation or the deception, etc. There can be a deviation from this rule for the purpose of reasonableness and fairness (Article 150 DCCP). The court must then indicate what circumstances have led to take such a decision.[81] As an example, irregularities for which no explanation is given or the improbability of the statements of the party who has introduced the document are circumstances that may give rise to such a reversal of the burden of proof.

'Alternatively, a court may resort to a less far-reaching measure: the so-called "improper reversal of the burden of proof". In such a case, the court provisionally presumes the non-authenticity of the document, on the basis of facts that have surfaced during the procedure, e.g.: by the document's appearance it is clear that the text has been written in several stages. On the basis of this fact the court presumes that the document is not authentic. It is then up to the relying party to disprove the provisional presumption of non-authenticity. This does not mean that the relying party has to prove the authenticity of the

---

[81] See HR 15 January 1993, NJ 1993, 179, RvdW 1993, 32.

document (that would be the case with a real reversal of the burden of proof), but he may suffice by giving another reasonable explanation for the text being written in different stages (e.g., the pen ran out of ink), thus invalidating the provisional presumption, without really proving authenticity. If the relying party succeeds in invalidating the presumption, it is up to the holder to really prove the non-authenticity'.

If a document is a private instrument, the DCCP lays down a special rule with respect to the division of the burden of proof. If the signing of a document is positively denied by the person against whom the private instrument provides compulsory proof, the private instrument does not provide proof as long as it is not proven from whom the signature originates (Article 159 DCCP). If the person against whom the instrument is invoked is not the person who has signed it (think, e.g., of a successor in title), then this person need not positively deny the signature. It suffices that he states that he does not recognise the authenticity of the signature. This means that the burden of proof concerning the authenticity of the signature rests upon the party that invokes the private instrument (the relying party).[82] At the time the government gave the following reason for this special rule on the division of the burden of proof with respect to the authenticity of a signature.

'If the authenticity of a signature is positively denied, the document on which the signature is placed usually does not give sufficient clues for a provisional presumption of the authenticity of the signature. This has to be investigated and must be determined with the help of other factual data'.

The notion appears to be that it is not very likely that a signatory will deny his own signature against his better judgement.[83] Thus, if a purported signa-

---

[82] See HR 28 February 1997, NJ 1997, 330, RvdW 1997, 65 and Summary Court (Ktg.) Deventer 20 February and 2 October 1997, NJ 1998, 267. There is caselaw, however, from which it is apparent that a court is free to deviate from this division of the burden of proof, based on the circumstances of the case, such as the fact that the purported signatory only denies the authenticity of his purported signature on appeal. See Hof Amsterdam 18 June 1998 PRG 2000/5480.

[83] The Royal Commission preparing the revision of the law of evidence expressly stated so: (in translation) '[...] that, as experience shows, only very seldom someone will knowingly repudiate his own signature'. Rutgers e.a. 1988, p. 149. See also Pitlo 1995, pp. 451-452.

tory positively denies his purported signature, the signature is presumed to be a forgery; even more so, because an instrument generally does not give sufficient clues to convince a court that the signature is authentic. Given this presumption, it is not unreasonable to lay the burden of proof upon the relying party, who then bears the risk that it might fail in meeting this burden of proof. Can this line of reasoning also be applied to electronic signatures?[84] If the unauthorised use of an electronic signature is invoked, the presence of the electronic signature in itself does not exclude the claimed unauthorised use. After all, since both the holder and a possible unauthorised user have made use of the *authentic* signature, its authenticity does not give any indication of a presumption that the signature has arisen from authorised use. In general there are many ways to use an electronic signature without having the authority to do so. Therefore, it is not unreasonable to lay the burden of proof on the relying party, especially if it has gained knowledge concerning the integrity of the signature processes. This fits within the division of the burden of proof as laid down in Recommendation 97/489/EC.[85] The use of a confidential code or similar proof of identity is in itself not enough to prove that it was the holder who used the electronic payment instrument.

One could ask, however, whether the use of biometric verification of identity as part of the electronic signing process compels one to take another stand. Does a biometrically verified electronic signature not prove signing by the legitimate holder of the signature? I do not see any reason to treat electronic signatures that involve biometric verification radically

---

[84] An electronic document signed with an electronic signature can, according to the Dutch government, be qualified as a private instrument, if the all involved requirements for functional equivalence have been met (Kamerstukken I, 2002/03, 27 743, No. 35, p. 10). Uncertainty exists with respect to the functional equivalence of electronic documents with written documents. The scope of the concerned provision on functional equivalence (Art. 6:227a DCC in Kamerstukken II 2001/02, 28 197, Nos. 1-2, p. 5) is limited to form requirements with respect to contracts. This leaves open the question of how functional equivalence is to be determined with respect to other electronic documents, i.e., electronic documents that are not contracts for whose validity or incontestability the law requires a written form (see Van Es 2002, p. 858). Possibly, the same requirements for functional equivalence apply, but this is uncertain.

[85] According to Article 6 section 3 last sentence Recommendation 97/489/EC, the use of a confidential code or any other similar proof of identity is not, in itself, sufficient to entail the holder's liability.

differently.[86] There are many ways in which unauthorised use can be made of somebody else's signature, even though biometric verification is part of the signing process. A few examples may illustrate this: the personalisation of the reference template could be incorrect: A succeeds, for example, in having his bodily characteristic registered in the name of B. The false acceptance rate can be too high. The holder of the signature can be careless, e.g., leaving the computer unattended after completing biometric verification. Somebody might succeed in hacking the biometric verification process. After all, the bodily characteristic is translated into bits and bytes and these are susceptible to manipulation. Although in practice this may not be easy, it is certainly not always impossible. A biometrically verified signature does not therefore provide irrefutable evidence of signing by the legitimate holder. Therefore, a division of the burden of proof in which the relying party has to prove 'signing by the legitimate holder' need not be unreasonable.

In practice, the actual division of the burden of proof may also depend on the facts that have to be proven and who is in the best position to produce such evidence. If, for example, something has gone wrong with the signature creation device that is in the possession of the holder of the signature, a decision to lay the burden of proof on the relying party 'tout court' may not be reasonable.

A small point of statutory law is the following. Above, we have seen that if the person against whom the instrument is invoked is not the person who has signed it (think, for example, of a successor in title), then he may confine himself to stating that he does not recognise the *authenticity* of the signature for triggering the reversal of the burden of proof (Article 159 DCCP). The problem is that Article 159 DCCP in its wording actually speaks of the 'authenticity of the signature'. It is clear that with respect to electronic signatures the authenticity in the sense of being the 'real' signature is not at issue. What is actually lacking is the authority of the signing person to use the signature. In this respect the text of Article 159 DCCP could be updated.

Once it is established that an unauthorised party has used a holder's electronic signature, the evidentiary value of the concerned electronic

---

[86] See also Van Kralingen e.a. 1997, p. 49.

document as proof of signature by the holder is reduced to zero. At this point, it is however helpful to clarify that the signing by an unauthorised person may not always free the holder from liability. As we saw in the section on liability, the holder may still be bound by the legal act that came into being through the intervention of the unauthorised person, because the law may protect the trust that the relying party places in the electronic signature. Such cases may very well come down to determining whether the appearance of the authorised use of the signature can be imputed to the holder. Facts that shed some light on this issue then become the object of the provision of evidence. According to the Hoge Raad, it is up to the relying party to prove that it can be imputed to the holder that the unauthorised person had obtained knowledge of the code (i.e., the means by which to bring about the electronic signature).[87] The Hoge Raad is willing to help the relying party in this respect in that it states that such an imputation may generally be presumed if the unauthorised person is employed by the holder or if he otherwise has a relationship with the holder that places him in a position in which he, more easily than random third persons, could have access. It is then up to the holder of the electronic signature to put forward and prove circumstances that indicate that he did not act negligently.

The DCCP does not lay down any special rule for a signature in a private instrument. Therefore, the burden of proof in principle rests with the party contending that the statements have been altered.[88]

Amongst the parties, a private instrument provides compulsory proof of the truth of the statements of a party with respect to the aspects that the instrument is meant to prove for the benefit of the other party.[89] The party against whom the private instrument is invoked may disprove the truth of statements contained in the private instrument (Article 151 section 2 DCCP). For the benefit of such disproval, a court may consider the statements to have been disproved on the basis of all facts and circumstances that are brought forward, such as, for example, facts that became manifest

---

[87] HR 19 November 1993, NJ 1994, 622, RvdW 1993, 230 (COVA/NMB).

[88] See HR 14 January 2000, NJ 2000, 236, RvdW 2000, 22, HR 21 April 1995, NJ 1996, 652, RvdW 1995, 96 and HR 15 January 1993, NJ 1993, 179, RvdW 1993, 32.

[89] See Art. 157 section 2 DCCP. A private instrument does not provide proof of statements if this could lead to legal effects that the parties cannot freely determine.

in the course of the proceedings. It is after all within the sole discretion of the court to attach the necessary evidentiary value to each fact in the procedure as it deems fit.[90]

Conclusion

When there is a disagreement as to who has placed an electronic signature, it is in principle up to the holder of the signature to prove the unauthorised use. A court may deviate from this division for reasons of reasonableness and fairness. The legislator does so with respect to private instruments: the party invoking the instrument has to prove the authenticity of the signature in the case of a dispute. This reversal of the burden of proof has been incorporated within the law, because it is thought unlikely that somebody, against his better judgement, would deny his own signature. So, if a holder of a signature positively denies his signature, this can provisionally be presumed to be the truth, even more so because a handwritten signature does not definitively prove its own authenticity, without examining other facts lying outside the signature. This line of thinking may very well also be followed with respect to electronic signatures. After all, from an electronic signature it is difficult to deduce without examining other facts whether it has been placed by the person who is authorised to do so.

---

[90] See HR 5 January 2001, NJ 2001, 612, RvdW 2001, 23.

Chapter 5
PRIVACY IMPLICATIONS OF THE USE OF ELECTRONIC SIGNATURES

Chapter 5
PRIVACY IMPLICATIONS OF THE USE OF
ELECTRONIC SIGNATURES

5.1 WHY PRIVACY?

One could ask what the point is in discussing privacy in relation to electronic signatures.[91] By signing, the signatory intentionally relinquishes part of his privacy. One could even say that the point in signing is to 'use' one's privacy and to convert it into a useful 'commodity' such as trust. After all, the relying party derives trust from the signature: he will interpret the sacrifice of privacy by the signatory as a token that he is willing to stand by his signature. The trust subsequently functions as an 'enabler' from which the signatory can also reap the benefits. From this line of reasoning, one could ask whether there is a function for the law to protect a signatory against the very, even intended, consequences of his own action. I think that there is.

By signing one reveals information about oneself and opens up possibilities to link information concerning the signatory. This is relevant from a privacy perspective, because 'knowledge is power'. The advent of electronic signatures opens up new opportunities to collect and process information on persons. An electronic signature is by its very nature electronic in form, and thus lends itself very well to automated handling, thus facilitating its collection and processing. An electronic signature is furthermore an instrument that links information together (an identity is

---

[91] Privacy is a wide notion. It encompasses spatial privacy, such as the inviolability of the home, physical privacy, such as the integrity of one's body, relational privacy, such as the secrecy of telecommunications or respect for family life, and informational privacy, such as data protection (see Schreuders 1998, p. 23). Here, only informational aspects of privacy will be dealt with. Informational privacy is the right to determine oneself what may be done with one's personal data.

M.H.M. Schellekens, Electronic Signatures
© 2004, ITeR, The Hague, and the author

linked to a statement); this pivotal role of a signature makes it 'interesting' information. The information that can be derived from electronic signatures may very well be reliable information. A widespread possession of electronic signatures may give rise to a development in which people in their daily lives are more often required to identify themselves or are requested to accept terms and conditions, merely because the means to do so exist. A web surfer may, for example, be required to accept by means of his electronic signature certain terms and conditions before access is given to a web site. Electronic signatures could possibly mean a new lease of life for web site disclaimers. Holders of copyrights could try to bind the users of their works to contractual conditions by having compelling them to sign – almost undeniably – with their electronic signatures. Possibly, a scenario will evolve in which situations that have hitherto been informal become more juridical. Persons involved are identified and contractual conditions are imposed. I am not saying that this development will inevitably materialise; much depends on user acceptance of both electronic signatures themselves and requests to use them. Signatories may take their responsibility and critically appraise what they want to sign and what not. But, technologically, the advent of electronic signatures makes the described developments feasible and if these described developments do occur, those who can easily be asked to sign may very well lose out if the present situation is taken as a reference point. These considerations do not of course mean that the advent of electronic signatures is all bad news. But it is necessary to reflect on the preconditions within which this development is to be received. The law of informational privacy thus has an important role to play in determining the way in which electronic signatures will be used in the future. Hereinafter, issues of informational privacy will be dealt with concerning respect to a number of technologies for electronic signatures. The Dutch law of data protection came about as the result of various European directives, Directive 95/46/EC being the most relevant. The Dutch Data Protection Act – Wet Bescherming Persoonsgegevens – lies at the heart of the Dutch implementation.

5.2 DIGITAL SIGNATURES

The use of digital signatures does require certificates that link a public key to an identity or an authorisation. The certificate contains the actual information about the signatory, such as his identity, his authorisations or a number that is uniquely allocated to him. These data in the certificate may very well make it possible to link the signature and the signatory to other information concerning the signatory. The digital signature itself is less significant as a key to link together information about the signatory, since each signed document yields a different digital signature.[92] It is thus only through the public key, as found in the certificate, that the digital signature can function as a key to link together various data about the signatory.[93] Therefore, we will here concentrate on the certificate and see under what conditions the data that a certificate contains qualify as personal data and what implication such qualification has for the handling of certificates.

5.2.1 Personal data?

What are personal data? According to Directive 95/46/EC, 'personal data' is any information relating to an identified or identifiable natural person (i.e., a 'data subject'). An identifiable person is one who can be identified, directly or indirectly, in particular by reference to an identification number or to one or more factors specific to his physical, physiological, mental, economic, cultural or social identity.

The definition of personal data contains two main elements. In the first place, personal data must concern data relating to a person. In the second place, the data subject must be identified or identifiable.

In order to find out whether the data in a certificate are personal data, it is first necessary to know more specifically what data a certificate may contain. A number of certificates can be distinguished:

---

[92] A digital signature is in essence the encrypted hash value of the document.

[93] Note that the second use of the word 'key' in this sentence concerns 'key' in the meaning it has in computer science, not in the meaning it has in cryptography. The 'key' here means: the attribute or attributes that render a record unique in a table or even in an entire database.

The envelope and server certificates
We have seen the envelope certificate earlier as one of the certificates offered by Diginotar. It is a certificate that identifies an organisation or an entire department within an organisation. It does not denote a specific person and is not a token of authorisation. The server certificate was encountered earlier when we spoke of Secure Socket Layers and TLS. The certificate identifies a server.

These certificates identify, in the first place, an object. Does that mean that they are not personal data because they do not relate to a natural person? Not necessarily. In principle they are not personal data, but if a person is specifically connected to the objects and he is reasonably easily identifiable, then the identification of the object can amount to personal data.

The authorisation certificate
This certificate does not contain the identity of a person; it does contain an authorisation, however. The certificate is unique because of the uniqueness of the public key or the uniqueness of a certificate identification number. This key or number can be seen as a number that is specifically bound to a person: the person authorised (the authorisee). This does not necessarily entail that the authorisee is identified or identifiable. So, only in circumstances in which the authorisee is reasonably easily identifiable can the key or number be qualified as personal data. This may be the case if the TTP records in a database to whom an authorisation certificate has been allocated. The TTP may want to record this information in order to be able to withdraw the authorisation certificate without the co-operation of the authorisee.

The identity certificate and the pseudonym certificate
The identity in an identity certificate is, of course, personal data. A pseudonym certificate contains a pseudonym instead of a 'real' identity. Is a pseudonym personal data? Here again, the pseudonym is indeed personal data if it is reasonably easily retraceable to an identified or identifiable person. In practice, some data are usually available with which a pseudonym can be traced back to an identity. The CSP may, for example, issue a pseudonym certificate if, and only if, he knows the real identity behind the pseudonym.

The mapping from pseudonym to identity may be stored in a back office database.

In the foregoing, it is assumed that it is always clear whether an identity certificate or a pseudonym certificate is concerned. That is not always the case. Directive 1999/93/EC requires that a qualified pseudonym certificate should indicate that the name mentioned in the certificate is a pseudonym.[94] For other pseudonym certificates such an indication is not required.

In practice, the consequence of non-indication may be that the pseudonym is mistakenly held to be the real identity. In such a case a pseudonym will be treated as if it were personal data. Once the pseudonymical character of the pseudonym is discovered, however, the qualification of the pseudonym as personal data will be reassessed: if the pseudonym can be retraced to the real identity, the pseudonym constitutes 'personal data'. Otherwise (the identity is untraceable), the pseudonym can generally not be qualified as personal data.

Theoretically, it may also be the case that the pseudonym is used so often that it acquires the traits of an identity. Then the pseudonym may even be personal data without knowledge of the real identity behind the pseudonym. Whether a pseudonym acquires the status of an identity is dependent upon the context in which it is used.

5.2.2 The processing of personal data

'Processing of personal data' means any operation or set of operations which is performed upon personal data, whether or not by automatic means, such as collection, recording, organization, storage, adaptation or alteration, retrieval, consultation, use, disclosure by transmission, dissemination or otherwise making available, alignment or combination, blocking, erasure or destruction.

The collection and processing of personal data by Certification Service providers is regulated in the Dutch Telecommunications Act and is stricter than would have been the case if it had solely been governed by the Dutch Data Protection Act. A certification service-provider that issues

---

[94] See Art. 11.2 Directive 99/93/EC.

certificates to the public may collect personal data only directly from the data subject, or after the explicit consent of the data subject, and only insofar as it is necessary for the purposes of issuing and maintaining the certificate. The data may not be collected or processed for any other purposes without the explicit consent of the data subject. Such explicit consent is however not required if the processing of the personal data is necessary for the investigation of criminal offences or if the processing is required by statutory law.

A number of issues arise with respect to the processing of personal data in relation to certificates. For example, it is relevant what data are to be put in the certificate, how the certificate is to be distributed, what its validity period is and what information is made available in case a certificate has to be put on a CRL.

What data may be recorded in a certificate?
As we have seen above, a CSP may only collect data directly from the data subject or after the explicit consent of the data subject. The data that are recorded in the certificate must serve the purpose for which the certificate is to be used. The inclusion of the data must have a reasonable relationship with the purpose of their inclusion (proportionality) and the data must be the least burdening alternative that serves the purpose (subsidiarity).

Looking at the different types of certificates, a certain potential for meeting the requirements is present: for some applications it suffices to have authorisations; the mentioning of an identity can then be omitted. Also the use of pseudonyms offers opportunities: a pseudonym can be used instead of a 'real' identity. Furthermore, an indication of the status of an identity – real or pseudonym – can sometimes be omitted. In a qualified certificate, the status must however be indicated in the case of pseudonyms. Care must also be taken with unique numbers, or other information that is specifically bound to the holder of a certificate; some numbers or information are more persistent than other numbers. A social security number or a biometric template are bound to the holder of the certificate for the duration of his life.

How can a certificate be distributed?
A certificate can be distributed in more than one way. The certificate can be 'handed' to the holder of the signature (or, to be more precise, the person

holding the device for bringing about the signature). It is then up to the holder to distribute the certificate to whoever requires it. This approach is preferable to publishing the certificate on a web site. The presence of many certificates in a public database may enhance its attractiveness for linking together different information about the holders. From a large group of people profiles could, for example, be made. In purely internal use of certificates, the certificates need not be distributed. For example, a bank is a RA for the public keys of its customers and subsequently relies on the signatures of its customers based on the registered public keys.

Finally, it must be remarked that by reducing the validity period of a certificate its usability as a means to link together information about the holder decreases, because the relevance of the data in a certificate is from a privacy perspective greater if the certificate is used over a longer period of time and for more 'transactions'. Its linking capability increases.

What should be published if a certificate is revoked?
If a certificate is revoked, the unique sequence number of the certificate is enough to identify the certificate as having been revoked. The cause of revocation need not be mentioned.

5.3   SYMMETRIC ENCRYPTION

In the case of authentication by symmetric encryption without a TTP, no information needs to be certified. Two parties share a key; they, and only they, know who the other party is or what authorisations the other party has. From chapter 2, it is apparent that an authentication scheme based on this form of using symmetric encryption is seriously impaired by the number of keys involved and the associated key distribution problem. Therefore, we will henceforth concentrate on authentication by symmetric encryption with a TTP. In chapter 2, three ways of setting up an authentication scheme with the help of symmetric encryption and TTPs were discerned:

- 'Messages' pass through the 'hands' of the TTP,
- a key centre distributes the keys, or
- keys are distributed with the help of asymmetric encryption.

In the first mentioned scheme, the TTP certifies the identity or 'authorisation' of the sender to the 'receiver'. For privacy reasons, it is desirable that the TTP only receives and certifies hashes of messages and not the messages themselves. In this way the contents of messages do not become known to the TTP. In order to demonstrate 'sending' by the sender to a third party at a later time the TTP must retain the keys it shares with the participants in the scheme. However, the message or hash – as encrypted by the sender – need not be retained by the TTP. He can send them to the receiver who can retain them as evidence. If the occasion of producing evidence will arise, the receiver can return the hash to the TTP.

In the case of a key centre distributing keys, the following scenario was considered. If A requests a key for communication with B, the key centre delivers a key to A with the certification that the 'same' key has been delivered to B and only to B. Likewise, the same key is delivered to B with the certification that it has also been delivered to A. A and B can now communicate without the intervention of the key centre. The messages or hashes sent between A and B do not pass through the hands of the TTP. Compared with the first scheme, this has the advantage that the TTP does not obtain an insight into the messaging between A and B; the TTP does not know, for example, when and how often A and B send messages to each other. For evidentiary purposes, the TTP must retain information concerning what keys have been distributed to what participants, so that he can provide evidence as to the key distribution at a later time, if the necessity arises. For this purpose, it may be enough that only hashes of the keys are retained and not the keys themselves.

In the third scheme, the symmetric keys are distributed using asymmetric encryption. The information that can be derived from the use of a 'symmetric' key depends upon what information is tied to the use of the 'asymmetric keys' with the aid of which the symmetric key has been negotiated. For the privacy-related issues, I refer to section 5.2.

5.4   BIOMETRICS: THE DYNAMIC SIGNATURE OR SIGNATURE-SCAN

As has been described in chapter 2, the biometric characteristic that is measured in the case of dynamic signatures, is the way in which the signatory signs. The result of such measurement is stored in a template, called the live scan. The live scan is matched against one or more reference templates. The result of the matching process is indicated in the document that was signed. The template of the live scan itself is not part of the document. From a privacy perspective, it is relevant to know how the verification takes place. Such verification can take place on-line and off-line. If the application for which the verification is needed thereby allows, off-line is preferable from a privacy perspective. This means that both the reference template is stored decentrally and that the verification takes place decentrally. An example may be the securing of access to a private key of a digital signature with the help of a dynamic signature: the reference template and the private key are stored on a hardware token – such as a smartcard or an USB token – that is held by the person whose biometric template and private key it contains. The signatory signs and the measured dynamic characteristics of his signature are matched against the reference template on the hardware token. If the verification is positive the hardware token gives access to the private key and the digital signature can be made. For other applications, however, it may be necessary to have the verification performed by a trusted third party, who centrally holds the reference templates. In general, the central storage of a biometric template is especially relevant from a privacy perspective. A biometric template contains data that are uniquely linked to the person of the signatory. These data stay the same for the lifetime of the signatory or at least for a long time (taking account of slight changes over time in the way somebody signs). The relevance of such data lies with their potential to relate data about the person together, e.g., used to build up a profile. The Dutch Data Protection Authority therefore advises against the central storage of biometric templates where this is not necessary.[95] In the case of CyberSIGN for Word, live scans, for example, are not stored after verification.

All processing of the biometric data must of course be adequately secured. From a privacy perspective, it is relevant whether the TTP stores data about the verifications of live scans that have been performed and, if so, what data are stored. Such storage could serve the purpose of a later certification by the TTP of the act of signing, the identity of the signatory,

[95] Hes, Hooghiemstra and Borking 1999, pp. 51-56 and p. 67.

the time of signing or other facts. What data the TTP is allowed to store is closely related to the certification services he provides.

If the live scans are not retained, the probative power of a dynamic signature comes to depend on the integrity with which the real time verification has taken place and the integrity with which the result of this verification is conserved. After all, due to the lack of the live scan, the verification cannot be repeated at the time of producing evidence. The non-existence of the live scan does have an advantage, however. If the live scan or other biometric template would exist and would have to be produced during the production of evidence in a court of law, the template may become 'public knowledge'. This may very well diminish the value of subsequent (and perhaps even past) biometric verifications involving the signatory whose template has become public. This risk is removed if the live scan simply no longer exist.

5.5   CONCLUSION

Privacy issues are relevant with respect to electronic signatures. Electronic signatures provide information about the signatory. The widespread possession of electronic signatures may mean that people will be requested to use their signatures in more situations than is presently the case. Both these possible inherent consequences of the use of electronic signatures are disadvantageous for the signatories. However, holders of electronic signatures are not defencelessly exposed to these consequences. Primarily, if and when the handling of electronic signatures involves the processing of personal data, it must comply with the rules of informational privacy. Secondly, holders of electronic signatures can critically appraise for what uses it is worth using their electronic signatures and what information they are willing to release about themselves if they do so. The latter does presuppose that holders of electronic signatures have a palette of alternatives to choose from. Based on these two considerations the following recommendations/conclusions can be formulated.

Users must have a certain freedom of choice
The freedom of choice can be elaborated as follows:

- Holders of signatures must be able to have more than one electronic signature.
- Pseudonym signatures must be possible.
- Signatures from which it is not recognisable whether they contain a real identity coexist with electronic signatures from which this is recognisable.

Reticence in the processing of personal data
The data in certificates or data that are stored by a TTP in relation to signatories must be governed by principles of proportionality and subsidiarity. More concretely, this gives rise to the following observations with respect to electronic signatures.

- Attention must be paid to what data pass through the hands of TTPs. Preferably, the messaging takes place without the intervention of the TTP.
- Verifications preferably take place off-line, i.e., decentrally.
- Identification must be omitted if the purpose of the identification can also be attained by anonymous authorisation. As a middle ground one can use authorisations in operational, daily processes, with the possibility of identification in rare incidents that require further clarification of the facts: semi-anonymity.
- Real identity must not be requested if it suffices to have a pseudonym or a 'name' of which the status (identity or pseudonym?) is unknown.

Chapter 6
CONCLUSION

Chapter 6
CONCLUSION

The purpose of the research underlying this book is to describe technologies for authentication and to explore what is the usability of these technologies for their users.

In the description of technologies the following structure has been made. Firstly, technologies with little or no attention to malevolent use are dealt with. Secondly, technologies can be discerned that try to ensure that the determination of the person who is acting (especially: signing) is sufficiently certain. As a special case, the digital signature is dealt with. The special attention is warranted not just because of its complexity, but also because it is a technology that has captured the imagination of many people considering setting up an infrastructure for on-line contracting. Finally, some remaining technologies are dealt with, such as cards and timestamps. They are not per se authentication technologies, but may often fulfil a helpful supportive role for authentication technologies.

The second part of this book concerns 'usability'. Usability has many facets; in this research, the usability has been approached from the legal certainty perspective. It is an important usability requirement for electronic-signature users to be able to foresee the legal consequences. Without legal certainty, the trust and security they hope to gain from the use of an electronic signature may very well be lacking. The choice of authentication technology may also be dependent on considerations of legal certainty.

Four clusters of legal consequences have been studied: the qualifiability of authentication technology as a signature under the law, the evidentiary value of an electronic signature and liability for the misuse of a signature in conjunction with the division of the burden of proof and, finally, issues of informational privacy.

M.H.M. Schellekens, Electronic Signatures
© 2004, ITeR, The Hague, and the author

Qualification as a signature

Directive 1999/93/EC builds on functional equivalence, but only to limited extent does it make explicit what the functions of signatures are.

In 'Digital signature blindness', three legislative approaches for the 'recognition' of electronic signatures have been discerned. In Directive 1999/93/EC the so-called two-pronged approach has been chosen. On the one hand, advanced electronic signatures based on a qualified certificate are named as an authentication technology that is 'for certain' recognised as a signature equivalent. On the other hand, other authentication technologies may qualify as signatures. Authentication can here be understood to be a general indication of the functions of a signature. The directive and its Dutch implementation do not make explicit, however, what authentication exactly is, or, to put in other words, what the functions of signatures are. In this study, six signature functions have been discerned, based on a study of the literature: authentication, identification, authorisation, integrity, originality and the cautionary function. With respect to these functions, both substantive and evidentiary aspects have been discerned. Authentication is an act by the authenticator by which he earmarks a document as being authentic and in doing so confirms its authenticity. The identification function of a signature highlights that a signature makes it possible to determine or verify the identity of the signatory. An identity may be one's name or other usual denomination. Authorisation may have several meanings, but with respect to signature functions the following is the most relevant: by signing a document containing a declaration, the signatory implicitly declares that he is authorised to make the declaration and to perform the associated legal act. Integrity indicates that data in a document have not been altered, deleted or supplemented, irrespective of whether this has come about through natural causes or through manipulation. A second meaning of integrity is that a document correctly represents the statements of the signatory. In this sense, integrity relates to correspondence between the will, the oral statements, the knowledge of the signatory on the one hand, and the (correct) representation thereof in the document on the other. Originality means that a document is an original, that it is not a copy. Finally, a signature has a cautionary function, which safeguards signatories from rashly entering into legal acts.

The signatory is thereby encouraged to take notice of the document he is about to sign.

How do these functions relate to the qualifiability of an authentication technology as a signature? For advanced signatures based on a qualified certificate the qualifiability is precisely described in Directive 1999/93/ EC and its appendices; so the functions are of less direct use. For other electronic signatures, knowledge about the functions is relevant for determining their qualifiability as signature equivalents. According to Dutch law, an electronic signature must, for example, be sufficiently reliable as an authentication technology. From the requirements with which advanced electronic signatures have to comply, it can be deduced that the European Commission sees the authentication function and the identification function as the core functions of signatures. Where the qualification as a signature is most relevant – i.e., a form requirement demanding a signature or a signed document – it is the form requirement and its rationale that indicate what functions are crucial for the functional equivalence of the electronic signature to the traditional, handwritten signature. So, between form requirements the emphasis can shift from some functions to others. Functional equivalence based on four of six functions may be quite adequate in the light of one form requirement, but insufficient in the light of another. This implies that some flexibility in the determination of the functions of a signature is desirable. Nevertheless, in order to determine the usability of electronic signatures it is paramount that clarity concerning the possible functions of signatures exists.

As a last remark the following can be said. In the end, the result with respect to legal certainty is not as good as it could have been. This is attributable to the unfortunate co-ordination between Directives 1999/93/ EC and 2000/31/EC that has given rise to the existence of a 'no man's land': the former directive does not deal with form requirements relating to contracts, the latter does not deal with signature issues. As a consequence the contractual form requirement of a signature has formally not been dealt with at all. This may mean that it is now up to the courts to decide whether the form requirement of a signature can be met by an electronic signature.

The limitations of authentication technologies

The approach of imitating traditional handwritten signatures with electronic signatures has its limitations. Some traditional functions cannot be performed by electronic signatures.

Although we speak of functional equivalence, an electronic signature is still something different from a handwritten signature. The concept of functional equivalence presupposes that the off-line world can be emulated on-line. Even more so, it is assumed that electronic signatures can perform the functions of traditional signatures by emulating the characteristics of these functions. That does not give rise to the question whether electronic signatures are really adequate for mimicking all functions of traditional signatures by modelling them on traditional signatures. There is at least one function of which it is questionable whether an electronic signature can copy the way in which a traditional signature fulfils this function: originality. With respect to the originality function in the law of evidence – originality is a token of authenticity – this is not so pronounced. But with respect to its function in substantive law – originality is a token of uniqueness – emulation of the off-line world is problematic. Originality is the ability to distinguish originals from copies. With respect to digital data, one could define original data as the first set of particular data that came about. One would however directly run into the problem that, in practice, this first set is indistinguishable from later copies. Timestamping may be used to record when the first set came about, but it does not really prevent copying; it does not prevent more copies from coming into circulation, laying claim to the same timestamp. If originality is really to be warranted it probably comes to depend on contractual and organisational measures. Bolero – the system for bills of lading – solves the uniqueness by originality issue by requiring that all communications pass through a central registry that records them and that is able to detect that a certain message is being communicated for a second or subsequent time. This means that it has legally become something completely different. Uniqueness is something that is no longer deduced from a characteristic of a signature or a document. There is a central registry that becomes the 'authentic source' for originality and uniqueness issues. The role of electronic signatures is in such cases limited to placing the authenticity of the message recorded in the central registry beyond any doubt.

From a usability perspective, one can remark that the electronic signature cannot itself perform the function of originality in the sense of uniqueness. Here the equalisation approach does not work and for the usability of the originality function, considerations concerning the usability of authentic registrations are needed.

A second remark with respect to the equalisation approach is the following. It may be that a signature can perform a function, while the function can even better be warranted by some means other than an electronic signature. This other means can then be used in conjunction or even instead of the electronic signature. The cautionary function of signatures provides an example.

Traditionally, a signatory knows that important legal consequences can ensue from placing one's signature under a document. Theoretically, this function can be performed on-line with the help of an electronic signature: the electronic signatory is aware of what he is doing and thus the cautionary function is realised. However, the question whether the signatory really is aware of what he is doing is perhaps even to a greater extent dependent upon the way in which the user interface has been laid out. For this function the off-line-on-line is not an adequate approach. Directive 2000/31/EC goes some way in requiring that a service provider makes available to the recipient of the service, effective and accessible technical means allowing him to identify and correct input errors, prior to the placing of the order (Article 11 paragraph 2 Directive 2000/31/EC). This shows that if functions that can better be performed on-line by technological measures other than electronic signatures are to be statutorily warranted, they require additional statutory provisions. This can be done by introducing new requirements that make the functions explicit and may then perhaps no longer be called form requirements. From a usability perspective, one can again conclude that an electronic signature in itself may not always be enough and that a broader approach is needed.

The electronic signature as evidence

Directive 1999/93/EC has laid a sound legal foundation for the evidentiary value of electronic signatures. However, the belief of prospective users that an electronic signature is a reliable means of authentication is something that has to grow.

A starting point of the civil law of evidence is the freedom of a court to assess the evidence. For evidence by electronic signature, this starting point has been retained.[96] What holds true off-line is here extrapolated to the on-line. The discretion of a court in this respect necessarily has implications for legal certainty. Absolute assurances concerning evidentiary status cannot be provided. This also holds true for traditional handwritten signatures. What is lacking with respect to electronic signatures is something which is difficult to describe: perhaps the trust that a signed document will provide the necessary proof is the description that comes nearest. There is, as yet, not a body of caselaw that lays a foundation for this 'trust' that electronic signatures are effective means for providing evidence. Directive 1999/93/EC only has limited means to address this lack of trust. The most important contribution of the directive is the symbolic value which it has; it places electronic signatures on the map as a viable alternative to traditional handwritten signatures. It does not so much diminish the freedom of a court to assess the evidentiary value it is willing to attribute to an electronic signature. Furthermore, Directive 1999/93/EC provides for the freedom to agree on the evidentiary status of electronic documents and signatures. Parties can then diminish uncertainties concerning the evidentiary value that is to be attached to electronic signatures.

---

[96] Exceptions are: the limitations on a court in assessing the evidentiary value in Art. 5.2 Directive 1999/93/EC and, additionally, in Dutch law the qualifiability of a signed electronic document as an instrument.

Electronic signatures and alternatives

For many transactions, the law does not require a signature. Technologies of which their qualifiability as a signature is uncertain may therefore provide viable alternatives for electronic signatures in the (relatively frequent) situations where legally no signature is required.

The law only requires signatures in relatively rare situations. In many situations signatures are used without any legal obligations to do so. In such cases they are used for the trust and security that can be derived therefrom. A handwritten signature comes at virtually no cost. From the cost aspect the decision to use traditional handwritten signatures may therefore be relatively straightforward.[97] Electronic signatures – especially digital signatures – do however often come at a cost. This means that the use of electronic signatures comes to depend on specific considerations of proportionality, subsidiarity and cost/benefit. Using simple alternatives or simple omnipresent technologies may in many situations be a viable alternative. The open structure of Directive 1999/93/EC may in some situations even allow low-key technologies to function as authentication technologies.

Liability and the division of the burden of proof

The possibility of unauthorised use is the Achilles heel of electronic signatures, especially if the technical measures taken to prevent unauthorised use build on the assumption that the holder of an electronic signature handles the token or knowledge that is the key to using the signature with due care. Biometric verification can be instrumental in diminishing the risks and the possible ensuing liabilities.

Liability questions are complex. That is, *inter alia*, caused by the number of parties involved and the intricacies of their mutual relations. Given the perspective of the usability of an electronic signature as used in this book, in dealing with the subject of liability most emphasis has been placed on

---

[97] Admittedly, maintaining a file of reference signatures and the consequent checking of handwritten signatures may be costly.

the liability of the holder of a signature flowing from the unauthorised use of his electronic signature. The assumption is made that an unauthorised user inflicts damage, by entering into obligations while pretending to be the 'legitimate user' of the electronic signature. If the damage cannot be retrieved from the unauthorised user, it may very well end up with the holder or the relying party, i.e., the party with which the unauthorised party sought to do business.[98] In Dutch law, the resolution of such a question may very well come to hinge on the question to whom – the holder or the relying party? – it can be attributed that the unauthorised use took place. An exploration of what duties of care have to be observed with respect to the prevention of misuse of electronic signatures has yielded the following result: the duties of a holder of an electronic signature depend in large part on what the holder can do to prevent misuse of his signature. It seems to depend less on the safety of the authentication technology used. There is no automatic correlation stating that the unsafer the technology is, the more precautions have to be taken. It is rather the scope for precautionary measures that a technology leaves open that is determinative. In short, measures that can reasonably be taken must be taken.

This finding could, for example, be used proactively to create technologies that require little precautions by their users. The use of biometric technologies is the prime example. Precautionary measures based on what one knows or what one has always require a degree of care with respect to the knowledge or its possession.

Privacy concerns

Counteracting adverse privacy implications of the use of electronic signatures for their holders is a responsibility of all the parties involved.

The use of electronic signatures has implications for the informational privacy of the holders of electronic signatures. The holders of signatures may become more transparent: information about holders can be derived from the signatures; the number of situations in which identification or

---

[98] Possible other parties that may be involved, such as TTPs, are not dealt with in this concluding chapter.

authorisation by means of an electronic signature is required may become greater.

In order to counteract adverse privacy implications, a two-tier approach is needed. On the one hand, holders of electronic signatures must be discerning about what information they are willing to release about themselves by using their electronic signatures. In order to tailor the information to the occasion for which the signature is requested, the holders of electronic signatures must have a choice of electronic signatures. On the other hand, other parties – such as TTPs and relying parties – must abide by the principles of proportionality and subsidiarity when processing personal data in relation to electronic signatures. A number of rules of thumb can be distinguished with respect to electronic signatures:

- Attention must be paid to what data pass through the hands of TTPs. Preferably, the messaging takes place without the intervention of the TTP.
- Verifications preferably take place off-line, i.e., decentrally.
- Identification must be omitted if the purpose of the identification can also be attained by anonymous authorisation. As a middle ground one can use authorisations in operational, daily processes, with a possibility of identification in rare cases that require further clarification of the facts: semi-anonymity.
- Real identity must not be requested if it suffices to have a pseudonym or a 'name' of which the status (identity or pseudonym) is unknown.

LITERATURE

AALBERTS AND VAN DER HOF 2000

B. Aalberts and S. van der Hof, *Digital Signature Blindness. Analysis of legislative approaches to electronic authentication*, Deventer: Kluwer 2000.

ANGEL 1999

J. Angel, Why use Digital Signatures for Electronic Commerce?, *The Journal of Information, Law and Technology (JILT)*, 1999/2, <http://www.law.warwick.ac.uk/jilt/99-2/angel.html>, visited in July 2001.

ATIYAH 1981

P.S. Atiyah, *An introduction to the law of contract*, Clarendon Law Series, Oxford: Clarendon Press 1981.

ATIYAH 1986

P.S. Atiyah, *Essays on contract*, Oxford: Clarendon Press 1986.

VAN BEECK 2001

W. Van Beeck, Public Key Infrastructure en de elektronische handtekening, E-identity, *Nieuwsbrief over elektronische identificatie* 2001/2, p. 1.

BURNETT 2001

R. Burnett, International Carriage of Goods (Updates Chapter 2), in: R. Burnett, *Law of International Transactions*, 2001.

CLIFT 1999

J. Clift, Electronic Commerce: the UNCITRAL Model Law and Electronic Equivalents to Traditional Bills of Lading, *International Business Lawyer*, July/August 1999, pp. 311-317.

DUMORTIER AND VAN DEN EYNDE 2001

J. Dumortier en S. Van den Eynde, De juridische erkenning van de elektronische handtekening in België, *Computerrecht* 2001, pp. 185-194.

ELLISON 1997

C.M. Ellison, *What do you need to know about the person with whom you are doing business?* House Science and Technology Subcommittee,

Hearing of 28 October 1997: Signatures in a Digital Age, <http://world.std.com/~cme/html/congress1.html>, accessed in 2001.

VAN ES 2002

P.C. van Es, Nadere opmerkingen over de Wet elektronische handtekeningen, *WPNR* 2002, 6515, pp. 857-858.

VAN ESCH 1992

R.E. van Esch, Het elektronisch identificatiemiddel en volmacht, *NJB* 1992, pp. 1073-1080.

VAN ESCH 1999

R.E. van Esch, *Electronic Data Interchange (EDI) en het vermogensrecht* (diss. Nijmegen), Deventer: W.E.J. Tjeenk Willink 1999.

VAN ESCH 2001

R.E. van Esch, Recente ontwikkelingen in het vermogensrecht op het terrein van de elektronische handel, *WPNR* 01/6443, pp. 373-381.

FABER 1996

D. Faber, Electronic Bills of Lading, *Lloyd's maritime and commercial law quarterly* 1996, pp. 232-244.

FORD AND BAUM 1997

W. Ford and M.S. Baum, *Secure Electronic Commerce, Building the infrastructure for digital signatures and encryption*, Upper Saddle River (NJ): Prentice Hall PTR 1997.

FRANKEN e.a. 2001

H. Franken, H.W.K. Kaspersen en A.H. de Wild (red.), *Recht en computer*, Deventer: Kluwer 2001.

HES, HOOGHIEMSTRA AND BORKING 1999

R. Hes, T.F.M. Hooghiemstra and J.J. Borking, *At face value. On biometrical identification and privacy*, The Hague: Registratiekamer 1999.

HUYDECOPER AND VAN ESCH 1997

S. Huydecoper and R. van Esch, *Geschriften en handtekeningen: een achterhaald concept?*, ITeR-Reeks No. 7, Alphen a/d Rijn: Samsom 1997.

KEMNA 2001

A.M.Ch. Kemna, De vraagstukken van bewijs en bewaring in een elektronische omgeving, in: Franken e.a. 2001, pp. 167-197.

VAN KRALINGEN e.a. 1997

R. van Kralingen, C. Prins and J. Grijpink, *Het lichaam als sleutel. Juridische beschouwingen over biometrie*, Alphen a/d Rijn: Samsom Bedrijfsinformatie 1997.

KUNER AND MIETBROD 1999
Ch. Kuner and A. Mietbrod, Written Signature Requirements and Electronic Authentication: A Comparative Perspective, *The EDI Law Review* 1999, pp. 143-154.

LARYEA 2001
E.T. Laryea, Bolero Electronic Trade System – An Australian Perspective, *Journal of International Banking Law* 2001, pp. 4-11.

LOEB 1998
L. Loeb, *Secure Electronic Transactions. Introduction and Technical Reference*, Boston: Artech House Publishers 1998.

MARTINEZ-NADAL AND FERRER-GOMILA 2002
A. Martinez-Nadal and J-L Ferrer-Gomila, Liability of Certification Authorities Issuing Electronic Signatures Certificates, *Electronic Communication Law Review* 2002, pp. 1-24.

NYKANEN 2000
T. Nykanen, Attribute Certificates in X.509, paper for the Tik-110.501 Seminar on Network Security in 2000, <http://www.hut.fi/~tpnykane/netsec/complete/toni_ac_complete.pdf>, last visited in July 2002.

PITLO 1995
A. Pitlo, revised by: P.H.M. Gerver, H. Sorgdrager, R.H. Stutterheim and T.R. Hidma, *Het systeem van het Nederlandse privaatrecht*, Arnhem: Gouda Quint 1995.

POULLET 1994
Y. Poullet, Probate form: From Liberty to Resposibility. Some Reflections on Continental European Law, *The EDI Law Review* 1994, pp. 83-100.

VAN QUICKENBORNE 1985
M. van Quickenborne, Quelques reflections sur la signature des actes sous seign prive, annotation to Cass. 28 June 1982, Revue Critique de Jurisprudence Belge 1985, pp. 57-104.

REED 2000
C. Reed, What is a signature?, *Journal of Information Law and Technology* 2000 (3), <http://elj.warwick.ac.uk/jilt/00-3/reed.html>.

RIHACZEK 1995
K. Rihaczek, Digital Signature Surrogates for Open EDI, *The EDI Law Review* 1995, pp. 229-240.

SCHNEIER 1996

B. Schneier, *Applied Cryptography. Protocols, Algorithms and Source Code in C*, New York: John Wiley & Sons 1996.

SCHREUDERS 1998

E. Schreuders, Waarden en regels: over privacy en de Wet bescherming persoonsgegevens, *Privacy & Informatie* 1998/1, pp. 22-25.

STORME 2001

M.E. Storme, De invoering van de elektronische handtekening in ons bewijsrecht – een inkadering van en commentaar bij de nieuwe wetsbepalingen, *Rechtskundig Weekblad* 2000-2001, pp. 1505-1525.

SYX 1986

D. Syx, Naar nieuwe vormen van handtekening? Het probleem van de handtekening in het elektronische rechtsverkeer, *Computerrecht* 1986, pp. 153-167.

THOMPSON 1995

D. Thompson (ed.), *The Concise Oxford Dictionary of Current English*, Oxford: Clarendon Press 1995.

VANHESTE 1997

J. Vanheste, *Het Internet handboek voor netwerkbeheerders*, Amsterdam: Addison Wesley Longman Nederland, 1997.

WINN 2001

J.K. Winn, The emperor's New Clothes: The Shocking Truth about Digital Signatures and Internet Commerce, *Idaho Law Review* 2001, pp. 353-388.

INTERNET LITERATURE

Introduction to SSL, <http://developer.netscape.com/docs/manuals/security/sslin/contents.htm>

APPENDIX

Consulted experts

W. van den Beucken (LCI Smartpen)

E. Hardam (PKI Overheid)

P.J.M. Kolkman (Senter, Ministry of Economic Affairs)

E. Noordhof (Enschede-Sdu)

C. Reinier (Philips Crypto)

INDEX

INFORMATION TECHNOLOGY & LAW SERIES

1. E-Government and its Implications for Administrative Law – Regulatory Initiatives in France, Germany, Norway and the United States (The Hague: T·M·C·Asser press, 2002)
Editor: J.E.J. Prins / ISBN 90-6704-141-6
2. Digital Anonymity and the Law – Tensions and Dimensions (The Hague: T·M·C·Asser press, 2003)
Editors: C. Nicoll, J.E.J. Prins and M.J.M. van Dellen / ISBN 90-6704-156-4
3. Protecting the Virtual Commons – Self-Organizing Open Source and Free Software Communities and Innovative Intellectual Property Regimes (The Hague: T·M·C·Asser press, 2003)
Authors: R. van Wendel de Joode, J.A. de Bruijn and M.J.G. van Eeten / ISBN 90-6704-159-9
4. IT Support and the Judiciary – Australia, Singapore, Venezuela, Norway, The Netherlands and Italy (The Hague: T·M·C·Asser press, 2004)
Editors: A. Oskamp, A.R. Lodder and M. Apistola / ISBN 90-6704-168-8
5. Electronic Signatures – Authentication Technology from a Legal Perspective (The Hague: T·M·C·Asser press, 2004)
Author: M.H.M. Schellekens / ISBN 90-6704-174-2